Endorse

MW00473526

"*Even if you never had the privilege oj* *personally, you'll find 'Ponderings from* ᴛʜᴇ ᴘᴀꜱᴛᴏʀ ꜱ ᴘᴀʀᴛɴᴇʀ ᴛᴏ ᴅᴇ ᴀɴ *uplifting, thoughtful and thought-provoking look into the heart of a woman who loved God, her family, and her church with everything in her. With deep wisdom born of a lifetime of searching God's Word in all of life's circumstances, Cheryl's legacy to us all is this daily reminder to seek God in everything, and then reach out to others. You'll find yourself referring to this little book again and again, and you'll be blessed every single time.*"

Genny Baxley – Vice President of Operations and North American Regional Director of Walk Thru the Bible

Have you ever entered a home and just by looking around learned a lot about the people who lived there? When you entered any of the parsonages lived in by the Hildbold family you always knew who they served. My former college roommate always had her Bible, pen and a notebook full of prayer requests close by when we attended Grove City College. It was no surprise to see them close at hand on her kitchen island. Her every wall was filled with cherished family photos and framed scripture verses. I remember when the children (2 boys and 2 girls) were younger. Chore charts hung on the walls, the reminders to be kind to others and to share Jesus were displayed just outside their bedroom doors. Scripture memory verses populated the walls on index cards as Cheryl prayed for her children to grow up to be a reflection of the Savior. Cheryl's living legacy are her children who are adults deeply rooted in their faith. Charlie, Carrie, Caitlin and Caleb are shining examples of lives devoted to our living Lord. Pastor Chuck and Cheryl -the Pastor's Partner- brought inspiration to others as they faced the challenges that life brings in raising a family amid the many changes that life brings. Be blessed by Cheryl's keen insights in bringing forth Christ to a lost world.

Jane Byham – College roommate and bridesmaid at Chuck and Cheryl's wedding

There are two verses that describe Cheryl Hildbold. Isaiah 40:31 says "Whoever waits upon the Lord shall renew their strength..." Daily, Cheryl waited on the Lord, and daily He renewed her strength! What a powerful living example Cheryl was and still is in our memories of her! In Matthew 5:14,16, Jesus describes Cheryl as "The Light of the world, who let her light shine before multitudes. Wherever she was, she instantly lit up the area! We saw her good works and great faith as she glorified the Heavenly Father. Yes, the Light of Jesus shone brightly through the darkness of her battle with cancer. So many others and I will miss her greatly. Forever, each of us will be strengthened when we face our own dark times in life! All because of Cheryl Hildbold's exemplary life and encouraging light of Christ in and through her!

> Ron Rand, retired pastor and author, honored to have seen Cheryl, the Light of the world!'

About forty years ago, I met Cheryl Hildbold. She didn't have an overwhelming personality or say amazing things. She simply lived her life in a steady, uncompromising, and loving way. Because of that, her influence in my life grew progressively over time. She was a beautiful writer. Many times, I urged her to collect her Ponderings and get them published. She never got around to doing so—probably because the more important things of life got in the way. Still, she had important things to say and did so in an understandable and unassuming way. Cheryl displayed the amazing grace that we all sing about. We sing it, she showed it. She lived a grace-filled life and died a grace-filled death. Hers was a life that inspired me to be a better Christian and to walk more closely with my Lord. Now, even though she has left this earth, others will have the opportunity to be inspired by her words and (as Scripture implores) to be provoked to love and good works (Hebrews 10:24).

May her words invade your heart and plant seeds that will bear fruit through your life.

> ~Dave Zuchelli—Retired Pastor & Author~

There's a song entitled, "Angels Among Us", in which a part of the lyrics go, "...And ain't it kind of funny that at the dark end of the road, someone lights the way with just a single ray of hope....to guide us with the light of love".

I believe Cheryl was one of those angels in my life. She had a voice that could entrance, enthrall and inspire. Cheryl's voice lives on in her Ponderings that will touch your heart as she touched mine. You'll find the stories totally relatable - some tender, some funny, always sincere and filled with "the light of love".

David Fredenburgh – best man at Chuck and Cheryl's wedding

To write about Cheryl Hildbold is to write about a warm-loving and caring person who from the moment one encountered her would understand these qualities about her. This was certainly true for us and became even more evident in over twenty years of friendship. Knowing Cheryl for that length of time, we had many opportunities to witness her love of and faith in our Lord and Savior, Jesus Christ. Cheryl had a strong calling to share her faith with others as she did through her newsletter articles which the title of this book is so named. There is no doubt in our minds that all who pick up this book to read will come to know Cheryl as the strong, loving, and caring Christian woman we knew. Moreover, and most importantly, the reader will come to know and/or grow closer to the One who loves us so much that He willing gave His life for us so one day we will reside with Him for an eternity as our dear friend Cheryl does now. God Bless.

James and Tammy Falcsik -friends of the Hildbold family

Proverbs 18:24b – "a friend who sticks closer than a brother (or sister)." Cheryl and I were friends for almost 50 years. We had several years together before college that cemented our friendship, and then our lives went different ways. Even though we didn't talk or see each other very often, I counted her as one of my best friends. Her "Ponderings from a Pastor's Partner" allowed me into her life. She was faithful to and consistent in our friendship. *Psalm 146:2 – "I will praise the LORD while I live; I will sing praises to my God while I have my being."* Cheryl was gifted with a beautiful voice and musical ability. She led worship for our high school youth group and it's obvious this quality carried her through until the end of her life. I'm sure she is front row center at the Throne praising God! *Deut. 31:6 – "Be strong and courageous. Do not be afraid or terrified because of them, for the LORD your God goes with you; he will never leave you or forsake you."* Perhaps this is the part of Cheryl's character that I respect most. In the midst of tremendous challenges, struggles, and pain, she remained strong (at least to those walking her journey from the outside). Through her times of weakness and discouragement she was confident of God's presence and grace in her life. I learned so much from her testimony.

Her Ponderings from a Pastor's Partner will truly be a blessing and encouragement for those who read them. **"And by faith (s)he still speaks, even though (s)he is dead." Hebrews 11:4b**

> Debbie Ludington Stocker -childhood friend and bridesmaid at Chuck and Cheryl's wedding

Ponderings from the Pastor's Partner

Cheryl Abrams Hildbold

Editing and formatting of this book provided by YCS Global, LLC, owners Steven & MaryJo Young. www.YCSGlobal.com.

ISBN: 978-1-09839-744-9

Table of Contents

Articles (Continued)

Articles (Continued)

Articles (Continued)

Forward

I get to write a love letter about my wife. The difficulty will be limiting it to these few pages.

Cheryl was an amazing woman, the absolute most Christ-like woman I have ever known. We first met at Grove City College, my sophomore year, her freshman year. I first heard her as she sang at a talent show at the beginning of her freshman year and her voice captivated me. I remember saying, "I need to meet that voice!"

We eventually started dating at the beginning of the second semester. At that point, she stole my heart and it has been hers ever since. We were engaged in October of my senior year and married three weeks after Cheryl graduated. I had already completed my first year of seminary, so after our wedding we moved to Middletown, Ohio for two years. Cheryl initially was hoping to be a Spanish translator at the United Nations, but those plans quickly ended and she eagerly took on the role of a Pastor's wife.

Over the course of our married life, we moved seven times and in each of those places, Cheryl became a vital part of the outreach and mission of the church. She was actively involved with various youth groups for many years while at the same time, raising four children.

One of her great passions was teaching. She loved to teach. So many kids loved her as their Sunday School teacher. And of course, her singing. She would sing in the car (most often while I drove, I would look over and see her with eyes shut, singing to the Savior she loved so much.) Our home always had music playing and she would be singing while preparing dinner. She sang when she took walks. She loved to sing!

The articles that you will read in this book will give you a glimpse into the things she loved the most: Jesus and her family.

Many of you reading these Ponderings will recall the monthly parsonage dinners she prepared for your birthdays and anniversaries. You will remember the annual open houses every year near Christmas for the local church and our community. Many of you will remember the programs that Cheryl led with our family for Mother's Day banquets and Christmas programs. I played the piano and she led the singing with our children. Many of you have in your homes crafts that she created and sold at craft shows.

She loved to take trips and took great delight at planning those excursions. She was very detailed and very organized and eventually taught me the importance of being more organized as well.

She loved math. She would say, "Math is fun." I never quite understood that and told her on many occasions that she was goofy. She always had a math puzzle going at home.

We both shared a passion for reading and our home would bear witness to that as her books occupied many more shelves than mine did.

We had a tremendous marriage and our love for each other never faltered. Not once. Early in our marriage, we struggled financially, but her organizational skills, discernment, common sense and faith made us stronger as a couple and as a family. And we would need that strength because April of 2016 was a turning point in our lives. Cheryl was diagnosed with colon cancer.

Even as she battled for over five years, her trust in our Savior never wavered. Through five different chemotherapies, one immunotherapy trial and ten surgeries, her witness remained strong. I was and continue to be in awe of her. What an example to her family, church family, friends and the medical community. We will not know how many lives she touched and helped until we leave this Earth.

Over the years, Cheryl wrote over 300 "Ponderings" and maybe someday we will compile the rest, but our family has selected these for your enjoyment. Our prayer is that they will do a few things: First, that you will get to know this woman that I love so much, possibly a little better than you already do. Second, that by reading these short articles, you will see the importance of a strong marriage and family life. Third, and most importantly, that you will be brought closer to the Savior who gave His life for each of us, the One that Cheryl loved and served throughout her life. His name is Jesus and you will read about Him all throughout these pages.

So, Cheryl, we will carry on until we are together again. I love you, Sweetie.

Chuck

My Personal Testimony

by Cheryl Abrams Hildbold

I was born into a home where my Dad was Catholic and my Mom was a former Baptist. When they married in 1949, they were going to alternate where they worshipped, but when my brother was born in 1950, we were a Catholic family. My sister was born in 1952 and I came along in 1958. We went to church every Sunday and said a memorized blessing before every dinner. At bed-time, I said another memorized prayer. I knew the story of Christmas and Easter and went to Catholic school through 4th grade...but there was never the mention of having a personal relationship with God.

My parents separated during the summer of 1967. I lived with my mom and my brother and my sister and since my mom had never turned Catholic, we stopped going to church. I also had to stop going to Catholic school because it was now going to cost us and we didn't have the money. So, I was adjusting to a new life without my dad and I was the new kid at a new school just trying to fit in.

My Mom remarried in 1970. My brother and sister no longer lived at home and I had to go to yet another new school. I was feeling very alone. I made some friends, but I always felt like I was trying to fit in. Most of these kids had gone to school together since kindergarten...I sort of felt like I was on the outside looking in.

On Easter Sunday, 1973, it was our turn to host the family meal. Our house was filled with Grandparents, Aunts, Uncles and Cousins...yet I still had a loneliness that I couldn't explain. I remember going outside and sitting on the porch and actually talking to God for the first time in my life...telling Him that I felt like something was missing in my life...not knowing that it was Him!

In the summer of 1973, I went to see the movie *Jesus Christ Superstar* and I was blown away. I saved my allowance and bought the record and listened to it over and over and over. I even recorded it onto a cassette tape so that I could carry it around and listen to it even when I wasn't home. In the late fall of 1973, I was walking up the road from our house, listening to JCS and crying. I felt lonelier than I ever had...despondent really. A car approached and it was my Uncle Howie on his way home from work. He asked me what was wrong and I told him that I was just lonely. He said, "I love you, honey and God loves you too and He is always with you." I had never heard that before...that God loved ME!

In the Spring of 1974, my parents and I had some friends that asked us to come to church with them. They asked us every week, but we always made up some excuse as to why we couldn't go. When we finally ran out of excuses, we told them that we would come...but that we were going to be shopping around for a church...just another excuse as to why we wouldn't be back for a 2nd visit! We went to a church in our old neighborhood... seeing people we hadn't seen for over 7 years...and it

"I love you, honey and God loves you too and He is always with you."

felt like coming home! Everyone was so welcoming and friendly. We knew we had found what we didn't even realize we were looking for...and we stayed! I got involved with the youth group and went to something called a "Coke Party" one Sunday afternoon. The youth leader stood up and talked about a relationship with Jesus Christ, which I expected to hear. But then a kid my own age stood up and told us that God loves us...the same thing my Uncle Howie had said. At that moment, I realized that this was what was missing in my life...the answer to my years of loneliness!

Let me back up just a bit. Remember how I said that I was always trying to fit in? Well, I was basically a "good kid". I didn't smoke or drink or swear. I didn't give my parents a hard time...but there's something I did that was worse than all of those things put together. I made someone feel worthless...on a regular basis. We had a fairly long bus ride to school. I was one of the first kids on and the bus was full by the time we got to school. One of the last students to get on the bus was a girl named Jackie. Jackie had a weight problem as well as some other problems that made her an undesirable seat mate for most of the kids. The bus always went around a big curve just before getting to Jackie's house and when it did, all the kids would spread out, making it look like their seats were full. Every day, Jackie would get on the bus and every day all the kids would look down...and every day, the bus driver had to make someone move over so that Jackie could sit down...every day...and I went right along with it...my way of trying to fit in!

Now back to the "Coke Party": I prayed the prayer that the leader told us to pray if we wanted to have a relationship with Jesus Christ...a relationship that would change our lives forever! The only thing was...after I prayed the prayer and opened my eyes...I didn't *feel* any different. The next day, Monday, I got up, got dressed, got on the bus, went around the curve before Jackie's house...and moved over, making room in my seat for her...and made eye contact with her, letting her know that she could sit with me...and my life was changed...just like that!

I gave my life to Jesus in March of 1974, even though I feel that God was calling to me long before that, and I have never regretted that decision. On the contrary...I've been blessed because of that decision. I've been married to a wonderful man of God for 40 years. We have 4 amazing children, 2 sons in law, a daughter in law and a daughter in law to-be who all love the Lord. We also have the privilege to be a positive influence for the Lord in the lives of our 8 grandchildren. Now, my life hasn't always been easy. Moving around as we do, I struggle with trying to fit in and often times feeling lonely...but never as I did before I knew Jesus...because He is always with me...and I know for a fact that He loves ME!

Three things that I would like you to take away from my story:

- ❖ Never give up on asking someone to church...eventually, they'll run out of excuses.

- ❖ Make sure that you are friendly and welcoming to the guests that we have here at our church.

- ❖ A good story always has to have a hero...and this one has two: Jackie for having the incredible courage to get on that bus every day and Jesus: the One who makes all things and all people new! Listen to God when He calls to you...He wants you to know that you are loved and that He wants to have a relationship with you...one that will change your life forever!

And one last thing...it's not enough to give your life to Christ, you need to make Him Lord of your life and do all you can to grow in your faith for the rest of your life.

I'm Thankful!

I was the apple of my mother's eye and my daddy's little punkin'. I was my grandfather's playmate and the recipient of my grandmother's homemade cookies.

From the time we are born, people come into our lives and help to shape who we become. I am so thankful for those who have crossed my path over the years and I want to share a bit about SOME of them...for there are too many to name them all!

I'm thankful for my Uncle Howie, who was a reflection of Christ to a girl who was seeking to fill a void in her life and for Fred and Lois, who relentlessly invited us to church until we ran out of excuses and went. I am thankful for Jim, who hosted a youth event where I accepted Christ as my Savior and for Randy, Carol, Dave and Lana at Bethel Grove Bible Church who cared enough about the youth to lead us in Bible Study, Sunday school, Youth Group...and even dared to take us on trips!

"Jesus Christ has immeasurably shaped my life and I am thankful..."

I am thankful for Cyndi, Pat, Kristen, Debbie, Jane, Nancy, Joice, Tammy, Linda and Debbie who have taught me what friendship is all about. I am thankful for my brother, Grant and my sister, Diane who are also my brother and sister in Christ.

I am thankful for Chuck who is an amazing husband and also my pastor. I have been encouraged and inspired by his teaching and preaching for 35 years. He also made me a mother and I am thankful for Charlie, Carrie, Caitlin and Caleb...the greatest kids ever!

There is one more person I'd like to mention and her name is Janet. Janet and her husband, Pastor John came into our lives 40 years ago and always treated us like a couple of their kids. Back in 1985, I felt led to write an article for our church newsletter, and I knew that Janet wrote one for hers, calling it "Ponderings from the Pastor's Partner". I asked her if it was okay if I called mine the same and she said that she'd be honored. Janet just recently passed away and I am proud to be carrying on her legacy.

Lastly, I need to mention how Jesus Christ has immeasurably shaped my life and I am thankful for all the people he has put in my path over the years. I can't even imagine who I would be without Him...and them!

Steps

Most of us take them. In fact, "the experts" say that we should attempt to take around 10,000 steps each day! Many people wear devices on their wrists to keep track of their daily steps. Our steps take us numerous places and they provide necessary exercise too. Our daily steps are a big part of the journey that we are on.

Recently, we took a trip to Atlantic City, NJ to climb the historic Absecon Lighthouse which is 171 feet tall. Their motto is "228 steps - One Amazing Journey". We also walked along the famous boardwalk, making our way down to the ocean as well. We took a lot of steps that day and, in my opinion, it was truly an amazing journey.

I love using my steps to climb up on things that are high, partly because of the beautiful view, but also because it makes me feel closer to God. I especially like lighthouses because of the noble service that they provide. They are a beacon of hope in a dark world...just as we're supposed to be...just as God is! As we live our lives, letting our steps follow in Jesus' steps, we are guaranteed to have an amazing journey!

"You are the light of the world. A city on a hill cannot be hidden...let your light shine before men, that they may see your good deeds and praise your Father in heaven."

~Matthew 5:14, 16

Toddlers, Teenagers and Tylenol

What do these three things have in common? Well, obviously, they all begin with the letter "T", but they are also all present in my house! In January, Caleb officially became a toddler, and may I add, of the "terrible two" persuasion. This month, Caitlin turns 13 and joins the ranks of "teenage-hood" along with Charlie and Carrie. As for the Tylenol, I have Infant Tylenol, Junior Strength Tylenol, Regular Strength Tylenol, Extra-Strength Tylenol, and even some sample packets of Tylenol PM.

Let me give you some reasons why it is important to have Tylenol when you have Toddlers and Teenagers. Now, obviously, if I have teenagers, I've been through this toddler stage already and so it shouldn't faze me, right? Wrong! First of all, no two children are alike, so you never know what to expect and second, I was a whole lot younger when I did this toddler thing before.

Here is a typical day with my children. Charlie and Carrie have to be out the door for school by 7AM. Caitlin by 7:35AM. Somebody sleeps in, forgot to take a shower the night before and neglected to tell us about buying lunch until after it is made. Someone else gets a curling iron stuck in her hair, can't find her left shoe and was in too much of a hurry to make her bed. Someone else didn't save time to take the dog out or to wash the newsprint off the table and can't understand why he can't drive to school that day.

As the last teenager leaves, I hear Caleb calling from his crib, "Mommy, come get me." I go upstairs and change his diaper and struggle with him to get him dressed because he always wants to stay in his pjs. We go downstairs and I tell him to play with some toys while I make breakfast. I put our food on the table and notice that he's no longer playing with his toys, but he is rearranging the CDs in the stereo. He wants to listen to the B-I-B-L-E, which we put on repeat for our entire breakfast. I top off my breakfast with two Tylenol and we go upstairs to change a diaper.

We come back downstairs and while I clean up the kitchen, Caleb decides to decorate the powder room with toilet paper. (Everyone always wonders why our T.P isn't neatly on the spool like it's supposed to be.) Next, we go to the basement to do some laundry. While I'm in the laundry room, Caleb is deciding which tape to watch, which is easier to do if you take all of the tapes out of their cases and arrange them all over the floor.

After we pick those up and choose one, which is always "Veggie Tales: Where is God When I'm Scared?" I decide to do some sewing. Now, sewing also includes spending time at the ironing board and while there, I check on the laundry and Caleb decides to go over and move all of the settings on my sewing machine and empties out drawers of lace, zippers and ribbon reels (which, of course, come unraveled).

"There Is A God And He Loves Me!

It's time to go upstairs, take two Tylenol and change his diaper. We go back downstairs to play with toys and read some books. Then, it's time for lunch.

While I make lunch, Caleb takes all the books off the coffee table and pulls a lamp over. We clean up, wash up and have lunch. We always take our shoes off and play footsie while we eat. Then, it's naptime! (There is a God and He loves me!) I change his diaper and rock him to sleep. No matter how long he sleeps, it's never long enough.

About the time Caleb wakes, it's time for the Teenagers to start coming home. After a quiet day with a Toddler, they can be pretty noisy! They come home and raid the cupboard for a snack because they are starving. They also haven't been able to listen to their music all day and so they like to all do that. All different music. All at the same time.

They're glad to see Caleb after all day and like to play with him. They play tag (Mommy is always base!) and hide and seek (Mommy is always the best thing to hide behind!) and Caleb loves it when Caitlin pushes him around in the Little Tykes shopping cart (doing donuts around Mommy is the best part!). All the while, I'm trying to get dinner ready.

After dinner, the Teenagers mostly clean up the kitchen while Caleb fills his pants requiring an immediate bath. Helping with homework is also part of the evening and it consists of Pre-Algebra, translating Spanish, studying World Cultures and correcting grammar for an English paper.

Finally, it's bedtime for the Toddler with the Teenagers following behind at various intervals. At that point, my time is my own. I can finally do whatever I want to do, so I take two last Tylenol, kick back with my favorite book and fall asleep!

Now that the story is done, I want to be honest with you and let you know that not all of these things happened in one day, but they have all happened at one time or another. I also never mentioned my wonderful husband who helps out with the kids whenever he can and also how much help the Teenagers are with the Toddler!

> *Psalm 127:3-5 says, "Sons are a heritage from the Lord, children a reward from Him. Like arrows in the hands of a warrior are sons born in one's youth. Blessed is the man whose quiver of full of them."*

I thank God for the four blessings that He has given us, that our quiver is full.

Christmas with Chicken Pox!

We'll always remember this past Christmas as being the one that we celebrated with chicken pox! Caitlin had a fairly mild case with most of hers being hidden under her clothes. Charlie's, on the other hand, were out in full force...so much so that we nicknamed him "Spot"! I wonder if it will stick? Carrie (as of this writing) escaped them once again!

With one week to go until Christmas, I was counting on those last three days of school to accomplish the last of my pre-Christmas tasks, but I found myself with two out of three at home all day and I spent more time scratching itches than wrapping presents.

We had made some extensive plans for the post-Christmas season as well...time to be spent with family and friends had all changed. But, we had each other. Once the kids were exposed, all we could do was wait. We didn't know for sure if they'd get them. We didn't know what to expect...how sick they'd be nor how long they'd last. All we knew was that we had each other...and the Lord!

When life doesn't go as planned, we can be angry or disappointed or even depressed. The thought of an unknown future can be scary...never knowing what to expect. But when life disappoints us or even frightens us, we need to remember that God knows all and loves us and wants the best for our lives. We need to trust Him; giving Him our fears and disappointments and know that the best future we can have is a future with Him.

So, as we start out this new year with its many uncertainties, count on the One who is certain...Jesus!

Happy New Year!

New Year's Plans

What do you do when something that's been consuming your every waking moment is over? How do you deal with the slippery slope of the downside that inevitably follows a highlight in your life? For example, how does the bride adjust to life without dress fittings and gift registries, guest lists and being the "Star of the Show" for a day, going to days that are filled with dirty dishes and dusting? How does the young mother go from the excitement of setting up the nursery and picking out baby clothes, choosing names and feeling the baby kick to having sleepless nights and days filled with dirty diapers and constant crying? What do we all do, now that Christmas is over with its parties and shopping, decorating and baking and "Old Man Winter" has seemingly dug in his heels for the duration?

Let me suggest two things that we need to do. First and foremost, we need to keep our attitude in check...think positively...and creatively! I don't know about you, but as wonderful as Christmas-time is, it can also be very hectic. So, as Christmas becomes a memory and the New Year begins, let's have an attitude of thankfulness for a slower pace and more free time! Secondly, find some activities to do that will utilize some of this new-found free time. This is where you get the chance to be creative...and remember...there's something out there for all of us.

If you're at the stage of life where you have children, plan a mid-winter picnic in the living room...spread out a blanket and make your favorite picnic foods. You can even help the kids make ants out of black construction paper. Look forward to Friday nights with homemade pizza and board games. Take turns picking a movie and definitely take time to curl up with a good book...and nothing says winter like playing out in the snow followed by hot chocolate with marshmallows.

If it's just the two of you...plan a romantic dinner (by the fire, if you're able) to make up for all of the years when you couldn't because you had kids!! Play a game that doesn't involve getting lost in "Lollipop Woods" or sliding down some huge chute! Make some special plans for when your kids will all be home...because you miss them when they're not here!

If you're on your own, invite a friend over for a game of Scrabble. Make plans to go out to lunch with someone once a month. Send a box of cookies to your grandchildren with a note written just to them!

Finally, no matter what your age is, look for ways to be of service to others. Take your kids to visit a nursing home. Find someone who needs help around their house or with the shopping. Make a list of people who would love to get a card.

The list is endless! Make your New Year a memory...and a blessing...to yourself, to others and to God!

Cut-Out Cookies

I t's February 12 and I'm up early, trying to make cut-out heart cookies to send to my kids for Valentine's Day! I feel a strong need to do this because I never seem to get cut-out cookies made for Christmas...too many other activities fill up our time...things like Church dinners and plays and special services, band and chorus concerts, looking at light displays and keeping up with Advent devotions and calendars...not to mention, our annual Open House. There are also the usual things like shopping, baking, decorating, wrapping and correspondence as well as the unusual things like a wedding this past Christmas!

You see, one of my favorite memories from Christmas past is making cut-out cookies! I loved rolling out the dough and fitting the cookie cutters on just so...like putting together a jigsaw puzzle. I loved watching my Mom mix up the icing and then helping to add the food coloring until we had just the perfect shade. Of course, decorating was the best and I looked forward to it each year.

I'm in a hurry because I have to mix up this dough, chill it, roll it out, cut it, bake it, cool it, ice it and package it up all by 4:30! So, I quickly glance at the recipe and begin to mix my ingredients...1 stick butter, 1 cup sugar, 3 cups flour...oops, I should've only added ½ cup sugar...oh well, I'll add another stick of butter and 3 more cups of flour and make a double batch. I add the rest of the ingredients (double amounts, of course) and can hardly mix the dough. It's dry and crumbling. I try adding a little more butter and even some water, but to no avail. I re-read the recipe...1cup butter, ½ cup sugar...and I realize...I had added 1 stick of butter instead of 1 cup! I wasn't sure if I could add 2 more sticks of butter (double recipe...remember?) to the existing dough, but on the advice of my Mom, whom I had called, I decided to give it a try. Long story short, I was able to add the necessary butter and the cookies came out great. I was even able to get the ones that I needed to mail to the Post Office on time!

Mistakes! We make them all the time! Sometimes we realize we're making them and we make them anyway, but usually we don't know we've made them until it's too late...and we have a mess! I thought I caught my first mistake (too much sugar) and so I doubled the recipe, thinking that would solve the problem. However, my <u>real</u> first mistake was not putting in enough butter, but I didn't catch that until I was up to my elbows in crumbling dough, forcing me to go back...carefully checking the recipe. You see, when baking, you have to follow the directions...you have to use the proper amounts of the specified ingredients...or things don't come out right!

Isn't that true of life as well? We go through our days in a hurry, thinking we have all the answers...until we make a mistake...and find ourselves in a crumbling mess...unsure of what to do in order to fix things! I made a lot of mistakes making those cookies...but I did the right thing by going back to the recipe, back to the directions. We're going to make mistakes in life, but we'll always do the right thing by going back to the directions, back to God's Word, where we'll find a recipe with all the perfect ingredients to make a life that, in the end, turns out...great!

Being Real!

One of my favorite stories to read to the kids when they were little was the one about the Velveteen Rabbit. It's the story of a little stuffed bunny that's given to a boy on Christmas. Compared to some of the other toys in the nursery, he's nothing special...in fact; he is snubbed by some of the more expensive, mechanical toys. He is befriended by an old skin rocking horse that's definitely seen better days. One day, the rabbit asks the horse what it means to be Real. The old horse explains that "Real isn't how you are made, it's a thing that happens to you." He goes on to say that, "When a child loves you for a long, long time, you become Real. Generally, by the time you're Real, most of your hair has been loved off and you get very shabby." "I suppose you are Real?" said the Rabbit. "The boy's uncle made me Real many years ago," said the Skin Horse. "Once you are Real, it lasts for always."

Throughout the years of raising children, our home has accumulated many, many stuffed animals. Some of them were more expensive or special than others...although if you ask Carrie, they're all special! But, not all of them were favorites. The favorite ones were the ones that had to go everywhere we went and had to be tucked under the covers along with each child when they went to bed. Let's see there was Dandy Lion and Big Bird, Grover and Reindeer...given in no particular order...see if you can match them up with Charlie, Carrie, Caitlin & Caleb! These once colorful friends ended up with wobbly necks and matted, dirty "fur"...they ended up Real!

Something else we've accumulated in our home is Bibles. Between here and Chuck's office, we must have an estimate of three dozen or so. We have everything from a baby's first Bible with a handle to an enormous one that's almost too heavy to lift. We have easy reader Bibles, study Bibles and Greek New Testaments as well as devotional Bibles for Men, Women, Teens & Kids. They range from inexpensive paper backs that the kids get free at camp to nice ones with leather covers.

The Bible I use was given to me for my 28th Birthday...we're not going to bother to do the math! Compared to some of the other Bibles in the house, it's nothing special...just a hard cover study Bible that's seen better days having been hot-glued and taped together. Many of its pages have notes written in them with many of the verses underlined...but I have loved this Bible for a long, long time and it has become Real. You see, all Bibles are special because they contain the Word of God, but not all Bibles are Real. Remember: Real isn't how something is made, it's something that happens to it. In order for a Bible to become Real, you have to use it. It can't just sit on a shelf or a coffee table looking pretty. When you use your Bible, its pages will become bent and maybe even torn. Their edges will become dirty and smudged. It will become very shabby looking...it will become Real. And, as you become more and more familiar with God's Word, you will develop a Real relationship with God and, well, it lasts for always!

Another Birthday

The third week of March is always a big week for me...it's when the long-awaited first day of Spring comes and it's also when I get to celebrate another birthday! Well, Spring has "sprung", so they say and tomorrow is the "big" day. I'm always ready and excited to welcome a new season, so I'm glad that my birthday coincides with that change in climate (since I don't look at those birthdays quite as fondly as I used to!).

I guess it's human nature to grumble about being another year older...I mean, even wise King Solomon did...just read the book of Ecclesiastes! But, did you catch what I said about it being "human nature" to grumble? I'm sure it's not in God's nature to grumble...and, as Christians, our goal is to be more like Christ. So, I'm going to try and be happy about my advancing age and in order to do that, I need to focus on the positive things about growing older and not on the negative ones.

First, with age comes wisdom! Now, I'm sure I've forgotten some things about Physics and Trigonometry, but I've learned so much about what makes life important... relationships! How we relate to friends and acquaintances, family and co-workers and,

"...what makes life important... Relationships!"

most importantly, God, is what life is all about! Second, with age comes experience! I've come to appreciate the things I've been able to do, the places I've been able to see and the people with whom I've spent that time. Memories are an amazing gift! Third, every day I walk with the Lord brings me closer to Him. Throughout the years, I've learned so much about His Word and what it means for my life...and the more I learn, the more ready I am to be with Him some day!

So, another Spring is upon us and I'm looking forward to all that this new season has to offer...flowers and sunshine and excursions that we take, whether in the car or on our bikes! I'm also looking forward to all that being this age has to offer...the privilege to be a part of God's amazing creation and the blessing to share what I've learned over the years with others...which makes growing older so worthwhile!

The Chore Chart

School is well underway now. The kids have learned so much, yet still have so much to learn. Speaking of learning things: Caitlin, who is now in first grade, is learning how to read. It's fun to listen to her sounding out the words and, once she realizes what the sentence is saying, she goes back and reads it again; this time adding the proper tone to her voice. This is an exciting time for her...for all of us. As exciting as this is, though, the "mommy" in me can't help but have a touch of sorrow mixed in as I realize that she's taking one more big step toward independence.

So many people often tell us to enjoy our children while we can because, before we know it, they're grown and gone. As each year flies by, I am finding out just how true this is. Fortunately, though, God calls us to look at the "big picture" and not to dwell in the past. While we can treasure these moments that we have with our children while they're young, we are called by God to raise these children into faithful adulthood. It's good to know that we're on the right track and heading toward that destination.

We have chore charts for our kids. Each day there are 12 chores they must do: grooming, making beds, taking care of clothes and dishes, etc. These must be done without complaining. There is also a list of optional chores: dusting, sweeping, taking care of trash, helping with laundry, watering plants, etc., that can be done to earn extra stars. Each star is worth a penny. Pennies are received at the end of each day. Each child has a goal to reach by the end of the week and if they're successful, they receive a bonus: stickers, a book, an ice cream cone, etc. They can also earn extra stars for getting exercise, helping someone with one of their chores, or doing something educational: reading, flash cards or something on the computer. As you can see, the charts are well-rounded in many areas...all a part of our goal to raise our children into respectable adulthood.

Another of the mandatory daily "chores" is to read their Bibles, for which they receive a star. We also have Bible verses on the wall and when they memorize one, they get 5 stars! This lets them know how important this is...no one other item is worth this many stars. We also have family devotions and of course pray each day. We pray with and for our children that God will put a hedge around them to protect them from the evil that surrounds them and that they will be lights in a dark world...shining for Jesus. This task is easier in the summertime: the kids are out of school and under our influence and supervision. We are there to remind them to pray before they eat and to treat others with respect. Once they're in school, they're away from home for 40 hours a week and we can only hope that the training and reinforcement we've given them is remembered and put to use. We feel that part of the training they need is to learn to deal with the world and its ways; to be able to discern right from wrong and to choose the right way...God's way!

It's a big job...raising these children to be faithful servants of God...but one that's well worth it!

Teach them About God!

From tying their shoes to driving the car...and everything in between, parents have a lot of teaching to do when it comes to raising their kids! I remember spending hours in the bathroom, reading countless books with my "toddlers in training" and I remember the "laundry parades" we had as we carried the sheets down to the washer. I remember watching them learn to hit the ball as they played "rundown" in the backyard with their Dad, but mostly I remember putting stars on chore charts each evening...listening as the kids recited the Bible verses that they were memorizing. Yes, we parents have a lot of things to teach our kids...but nothing is more important than teaching them about God!

Now we have a sweet little granddaughter...who lives 19 hours away! Thankfully, she has two wonderful parents who are busy teaching her all the things she needs to know...especially about God! We're hoping that they don't always live so far away, but for now we want to make sure that Emily knows us and knows how much we love her. We get to visit in person several times a year and we also spend time talking on Skype (a means of communicating with cameras on the computer). We get to see her and she gets to see us while we're talking. We've watched her open gifts that we've sent and I even read her bedtime stories. We have some of the same books and so I read my copy while her parents turn the pages of theirs! It's a good way for her to get to know us even though we can't always be together!

We also feel it's important that she hear about God from us as well. We've always been thankful when others have stepped in and shared their faith with our kids so that they weren't just hearing about God from us. Ever since before Emily was born, I've been making and sending cards to her for all kinds of holidays and occasions. We always talk about God in the cards. A couple of years ago, we gave her a big fancy box to keep all of her cards in. Even though she's too young to understand everything now, we're hoping that as she grows, she'll think to look back through those cards and she'll see how much "Nana & Papa" love her, but also how much God loves her too!

Deuteronomy 6:5-9 says, "Love the Lord your God with all your heart and with all your soul and with all your strength. These commandments that I give you today are to be upon your hearts. Impress them on your children. Talk about them when you sit at home and when you walk along the road, when you lie down and when you get up. Tie them as symbols on your hands and bind them on your foreheads. Write them on the doorframes of your houses and on your gates."

Patience

Patience...one of the most elusive qualities in our culture today...we don't want to wait for anything...we want what we want...and we want it NOW!

There's a constantly-changing market out there for things to help us with our lack of patience and with each improvement, these items get faster and faster...thus indulging our impatience all the more. We couldn't wait to make phone calls, so now we carry them everywhere we go. We couldn't wait to get home to use our computers, so now they're on our phones. I remember when it took months, weeks or at the very least one hour to view our photos...now we can take them with, you guessed it, our phones and post them instantaneously on the internet for all to see! We can make a dinner of roast beef, mashed potatoes and steamed carrots in our microwaves in under 20 minutes...and they taste pretty close to a home-cooked meal that can take hours to make. Now don't get me wrong...these advancements are amazing and very useful and, yes...I have a smart phone...but there's something to be gained from waiting...patience!

To be patient, according to Webster, is to be steadfast despite opposition, difficulty or adversity. So, from the world's viewpoint, patience is something that can help us get through the hard times or, more exactly, help us to maintain who we are and what we stand for even when the world seems to be crashing down upon us.

According to God, patience is a highly praised, much encouraged virtue. In the Old Testament, we read that "patience is better than pride" (Ecclesiastes 7:8) and that "a patient man has great understanding" (Proverbs 14:29). In the New Testament, we find that "love is patient and kind" (1 Corinthians 3:4) and that patience is part of the Fruit of the Spirit (Galatians 5:22). In Colossians 3:12, we read that we are to "clothe ourselves with compassion, kindness, humility, gentleness and... patience".

As the things of man get faster and more frantic, the things of God stay the same. It takes anywhere from 8-14 weeks until you can eat that first sweet ear of corn after you plant it and when you find out that you're going to have a baby, it still takes approximately 9 months before you can meet your little blessing and it'll be years before the seedlings that you planted actually form that natural fence around your property.

Patience...don't let it elude you...learn to wait... "for they that wait upon the Lord shall renew their strength, they shall mount up with wings like eagles, they shall run and not grow weary, they shall walk and not faint." (Isaiah 40:31)

Memories!

They can stir up all sorts of emotions. We all have good ones and bad ones. Some are better off forgotten. Some are...priceless!

I'm talking about memories...and I strongly believe that if we focus on the good ones, the bad ones will tend to fade away. But good or bad, our memories all serve a purpose...they tell the story of life...our life here on earth.

As I sit in my living room, I realize that I am surrounded by good memories. I see souvenirs from places that I've loved visiting and photographs of our children and grandchildren...and the chapel where we got married. I see books that I've enjoyed reading and my grandmother's writing desk. I see *my* guitar and *Chuck's* piano. From where I sit, I can look into the dining room and see the table where we've shared family meals and entertained guests for 33 years. I see memories...so sweet and cherished.

As Easter approaches, I think about the disciples and the memories that they collected over their 3 years with Jesus. They see the hillside where Jesus taught and fed the 5,000. They see the Sea of Galilee where Jesus calmed the storm and walked on the water. They see the Temple that Jesus cleared out and where He also preached. They see the house where the roof was removed so that a friend could be healed and they walk along the road to Bethany where Lazarus was raised from the dead. They see memories...so awesome and amazing.

But then they see the garden and the courtyard. They see the beating and the crown of thorns. They see the cross and the hill called Golgotha. They see memories...the kind that haunt you during the day and fill your dreams at night.

They see memories

If the disciples were to follow my advice, they would focus on those good memories, hoping that the bad ones would eventually fade away. And that's what they were probably trying to do...when everything changed. Jesus came back. He arose...and set them on a course for making all new memories...some good and some bad...but all serving the same purpose...they tell the story of eternal life...our better life here on earth and the hope and promise of a future with only good memories...a future with God!

They Grow Up Fast!

Spring is here! When this time of year comes, I look forward to the time when school lets out and the kids are all mine again. No homework, no strict bed-time, no tests to study for! I like to make plans of the things that we'll do together as a family.

Some of the things we'll do will be expensive, like trips to Idlewild Park or our vacation at Rehoboth Beach, and those will be great times. However, I often find that some of the best times we have don't cost a thing (or very little)! All the kids like to make things in the kitchen, especially cookies! They like to set up lemonade stands and sell homemade items, like sun-catchers and potholders. Quite the entrepreneurs!

They love it when we gather around the table for a game of "LIFE", "YAHTZEE" OR "RUMMY CUBE". They like it when Chuck and I join in on the things that they like to do like riding bikes, taking walks and even occasionally roller blading! Caitlin enjoys "tea time" with Daddy and Carrie likes me to provide two extra hands to hold up all the Barbie dolls. Charlie enjoys telling anyone who will listen about all of his baseball cards. The girls love picnics on the sandbox and they all like playing rundown in the backyard with Dad. Group backrubs are a popular favorite! But, I'll have to say that probably the thing that they enjoy the most is when we tell them about when they were little...funny things they said and did.

These are the times that memories are made of. May you be inspired to make some memories this spring and summer because the saying is so true: "They grow up so fast!" Enjoy them!

Plastic Grocery Bags!

They are everywhere! We save them, we reuse them, we recycle them. Sometimes they get away from us. They blow across fields, they get caught in trees, they find their way out onto the highway.

The other day, we were driving along the Lincoln Highway (Rt. 30) and I saw a bag blowing across the road. The wind was carrying it somewhat, but it was mostly the moving vehicles that were responsible for the erratic motion of the bag.

As I watched that bag being blown around and run over, I realized that its only hope was if someone took the time to catch it, rescue it, save it from its purposeless fate. But no one seemed to care. No one felt that the bag had any value.

Thankfully, it was just a bag...but I think that there are a lot of people who are experiencing the same fate. People are being blown around by so many different "winds of teaching". They are told that their value is in their net worth. They are told that in order to be accepted by society, they need to have a certain body type and wear the right clothes. They are told to be tolerant of all lifestyles...even when they know that those lifestyles don't reflect God's perfect design.

People are being run over by a society that has no values and they are left with a purposeless fate. They need someone to take the time to care about them, to rescue them and to save them.

God, in His perfect design, has made that salvation possible through Christ's death on the cross...but He wants us to tell those lost, purposeless people about it! Paul tells us in Ephesians 4 that we are to be maturing in our faith so that we will no longer be tossed back and forth by the waves and blown here and there by every wind of teaching. Instead, we are to speak the truth in love!

It's good to recycle plastic bags...it's essential to speak God's truth in love to the lost around you!

We All Lose Things

We all lose things. Sometimes, we lose something important, but most of the time what we lose is trivial. When you lose your wallet, that's pretty important. When one of your socks has disappeared into the "dryer dimension", it's not that big of a deal.

Sometimes we find what we've lost, sometimes we don't, and sometimes, we can't. Sometimes, we search diligently for them and other times, they just "turn up" when we least expect them to. For instance, a few years ago, I lost my engagement ring in our car. At first, we searched diligently, but to no avail. After months of periodically searching, never giving up hope, but not realistically expecting to find it either, it was found, nine months later. Needless to say, I was ecstatic! Caleb has a toy train that came with three cars, three "animal passengers" and a conductor. The conductor was lost almost immediately (2 ½ years ago) and to this day has not been found. I'm sure that Caleb will be thrilled if that conductor ever shows up, but in the scheme of things, it's not that important. If a young girl (or boy!) loses her/his virginity, they can't find it again. It remains forever lost to them. If we lose a friend or loved one to death, we can't get them back. However, it is possible to see them again someday in Heaven if that person was a Christian and we are too.

Jesus talked a lot about lost things in the Gospels. In Luke 15, He tells us parables (stories) about a lost sheep, a lost coin, and a lost son. Although these stories are quite different from one another, they hold to a central message: we are all lost until Jesus finds us and we find salvation through Him. In Matthew 10: 39b we read "...whoever loses his life for my sake will find it." In other words, only when we give our lives over to Christ, will we find real life: eternal life in Heaven.

So, when you're wondering where that game piece went to or frantically searching for two socks that match...when you're looking for your car keys, do you ever breathe a little prayer and ask God to help you find them? I do! After all, God knows everything, right? So, He must know where our missing items are! Those kinds of prayers are fine, but make sure you take the time to pray the most important prayer you'll ever pray: the one where you admit that you're lost and need to find Jesus. And He will answer your prayer and all of Heaven will rejoice that you've been found!

The Night Light

We have a night light in the upstairs hallway. It's one of those light-sensitive ones that comes on automatically when it's dark enough. I've noticed that when you walk by it, even in broad daylight, it flickers on during the brief moment in which a shadow is cast over it. The other day when that happened, I thought about how we should be like that light. When darkness surrounds us and evil over-shadows us, we need to shine our light.

In Matthew, chapter 5, Jesus tells us that we are the light of the world and that we aren't to hide our light. We are to "let our light shine before men..." When trouble comes, we shouldn't run and hide, we should stand tall, allowing the light of Jesus to shine from within us!

Another neat thing about this night light is that it never "knows" when the darkness is coming. It simply stands ready for the task. Of course, in order for it to do its job, it must be plugged into an energy source and have a working light bulb in it. We too never know when darkness will come into our lives, so we must always be ready to shine our lights. We need to be plugged into our energy source, that is, the Holy Spirit. He is the source of our light. We draw upon Him when we pray, read the Word, and attend Sunday school and worship regularly. As for the working light bulb...we must have an active, working faith. We must have an outlet for the energy that we receive. Jesus likens us to a city on a hill, whose light cannot be hidden. We need to be proud and excited about our faith, not apologetic. We need to be witnesses for Christ in our homes, workplaces, school and everywhere we go.

So, as the song goes, let's "shine our lights 'til Jesus comes". That's quite a lesson from a little night light!

The Rabbit Died!

I thought I'd take this opportunity to share some news with all of you. To coin a familiar phrase: "The Rabbit Died!"

We've all heard that God works in mysterious ways and that blessings often come in disguise. Life isn't always as we plan it to be and we never know the "turns" we will take on the road of life. It's important, when these unexpected changes occur, to trust in the Lord...knowing that He has our best interest in mind. In Romans 8:28, we read that "...all things work together for good, to those who love God, to those who are called according to His purpose."

Just when you think you have life all figured out: a loving husband, a car for each of you to drive, three wonderful children, three cuddly pets and a home in which to share it all, you come to a "detour" in the road of life, the Rabbit dies and things change. Yes, I had an accident and "killed" our Volkswagen Rabbit. In short, I took a bad "turn" on the road of life, but God hid many blessings in the disaster.

1. Charlie and I were unhurt.
2. We were able to find another car...11 years newer and 130,000 less miles on it!
3. Even with no collision, we received $2,500 for the "dead" Rabbit and were able to pay cash for the "new" car.
4. We're _not_ expecting a 4th child! Where did you ever get that idea?

Eat Your Words

Did you ever say something and wish you hadn't? Of course, we all have at one time or another. Sometimes we say things in anger or in haste and we wish that we could take back our words, especially when those words have hurt someone. Other times, we say those words that invariably come back to "haunt" us. For instance, just the other day, I commented to Chuck how nicely the kids were playing together and no sooner had the words escaped my mouth that I heard a scream escape one of theirs.

Each month, I write this article for our newsletter and I am honored when people tell me that they enjoy it. I would have to say that of all the articles I've written, the one I wrote for March '98 got the most comments ever. Let me refresh your memory or sum it up for you. In February, I totaled our Volkswagen Rabbit and as I talked about this in my article, I made mention of the rabbit "dying". This was meant to be a play on words, likening my incident to a positive pregnancy test. In the end, I assured our readers that I was <u>not</u> expecting!

Now, this is one of those times when harmless words come back to "haunt" you and I am currently eating my words because, as most of you know, the rabbit did die and we are indeed expecting! My words in March may have been clever, but God is so much more clever than I and He obviously has something wonderful in mind and we are honored that He chose us to bring this miracle about!

PS – Be careful what you say: Eating your words may leave a funny taste in your mouth!

Setting an Example

Many of us have been followed by a member of the police force. You know the feeling: you're driving along, minding your own business and all of the sudden, you look in your mirror and see...a squad car. You check your speed, you check your seatbelt, you turn the music down, you check your mirror again...looking for lights, waiting for the siren to sound...and then, it doesn't. As soon as he gets the opportunity, he passes you and is gone from your life and you breathe a sigh of relief.

The other day, I was on my way to pick Caleb up from Pre-School and I was not followed by the police, but I found myself following him. I was following a car with the appropriate car lengths between us and a squad car pulled out from a side road in between the other car and myself, causing me to apply my brakes. That's one mark! I slowed down so that there would be a sufficient amount of space in between the squad car and myself, noting that he failed to do the same. He was definitely tailgating the car in front of him. That's two marks! When we finally came to a passing zone (not just dotted lines, but a whole extra lane), he flew past the car in front of him and within seconds, was out of sight. No lights, no siren, no apparent emergency. That's three marks!

In my nearly 30 years of driving, I've seen many people do these exact same things and have never given it much thought. That day, though, I was watching. I found myself wondering what kind of example he was setting for the rest of us. He was doing things for which he'd no doubt pulled people over.

However, before we get too hard on this guy, what kind of example are we as Christians setting for those who are not? Do we curse or use certain unmentionable hand gestures when someone cuts us off in traffic? Do we laugh at the off-color joke that's told in the lunchroom at work? Do we join in when some poor kid is the object of everyone's ridicule at school?

Does just about any other activity that comes along on a Sunday morning take precedence over going to Sunday school and Worship? Are our days too busy to spend some time with God? The questions: endless. The answers: embarrassing. The solution: God's Word. In Leviticus 11:44, we are called to be holy because God is holy. In Philippians 2:5 we are told that our attitude should be the same as that of Christ Jesus. In Philippians 1:27, we are told that whatever happens, we should conduct ourselves in a manner worthy of the gospel of Christ.

Remember, people are watching us and they need to see that Christ makes a real difference in our lives – a difference that they want for themselves. This holiday season and in this New Year, may we be beacons in the night, lighting the way to Christ.

In the Presence of God

I watched as he knelt to take communion. His movements were labored and noticeably painful. He bowed his head in prayer and received the bread and juice. It was obviously even more of an effort to stand back up...but he walked away with a look of satisfaction and peace. Being in the presence of God was worth the difficulty he'd gone through to get there. He bore his infirmities in silence, making no one aware of his circumstances. I just happened to be looking in the right direction at the right time...and I prayed for him.

This crazy season of Christmas is once again upon us and I so desperately want to make sure we celebrate the real meaning of Christmas and not get side-tracked with all the other stuff out there!

So, let's go back in time to a woman who made a difficult journey in order to be in the presence of God. Of course, I'm talking about Mary. She was not only expecting; she was almost ready to deliver. She and Joseph had to make the trip from Nazareth to Bethlehem to register for the census. The trip was 70 miles as the crow flies, but was probably more like 90 for them as they climbed in elevation over 1,300 feet as well. At walking pace, it would've taken them more than a week to cover that distance and height. I don't know how comfortable their beds were at home, but I'm sure there wasn't a lot of comfort along those mountain passes and whether she was walking or riding a donkey, she must have been exhausted! To top it all off, she wasn't even rewarded for her long journey with a nice bed at a hotel...she was offered a smelly, dirty stable...and then the baby came. The Bible doesn't share Mary's reaction to all of this. We don't know if she complained or whined, but we do know that at other times, she pondered things in her heart. For Mary, being in the presence of God made the long, hard journey and the undesirable living conditions worthwhile.

Life isn't always easy...not enough money, not enough time, poor health, no friends, no family...but if we focus on being in the presence of God...at Christmas and all year long, the difficult journey will be worthwhile.

I See You!

S o, I'm putting the finishing touches on Chuck's haircut and still haven't gotten one of those capes that "real" hairdressers use and so he is covered with hair. As he heads for the door to go out on the porch to "shake off", I laugh and mention that maybe our neighbor will be out there and see him in the boxers that he's wearing. When Charlie moved to Florida, he left behind some of his clothes, among which was a pair of white boxers with red hearts all over them...appropriate attire for a messy haircut. Checking to see that the coast was clear, he ran outside...just as the lady two doors over (who happens to be his secretary!) came out of her garage calling, "I SEE YOU!" You never know who's going to be watching!

I can still hear my Senior High Sunday School teacher telling the class how we never know who's watching us and, therefore, we always need to be mindful of our Christian witness. For the young reader or the un-churched person, that could be a very confusing statement, so let me put it another way. I know of a pastor who's often been known to say, "Remember who you are!" As Christians, we are children of the King. We are to live our lives in such a way that we reflect Christ. If we claim to be Christians, we can be sure that people will be watching us...for various reasons. Some may watch us to see if we slip up, make a mistake. Others may want to know if our actions go along with our words. Still others may be looking to see if our relationship with Christ makes any difference in our lives...because maybe then, He could make a difference in their lives too! And that's what it's all about...showing people Jesus so they want to know Him too.

So, this Christmas and into the New Year, may we find Jesus...and may people find Jesus in us. May God's love be the gift that we're giving this year...and may we wear our hearts on our sleeves (as well as our boxers!) Merry Christmas and Happy New Year!

Mary's Baby

Well, Carrie is about ½ of the way through her pregnancy. I often find myself thinking about the things that she's experiencing and I can't help but think back to my own...hearing that strong and steady heartbeat for the first time...feeling that little kick...wondering if it's going to be a boy or a girl. And then when we brought them home...realizing that things were never going to be the same...rocking them to sleep and then checking on them a dozen times each night to make sure that they were still breathing...wondering what they were going to grow up to be and praying that, above all, they would be a man or woman after God's own heart. It seems like a lifetime ago, and yet, it seems like only yesterday...they grow up so fast!

As Christmas approaches, my thoughts also turn to another girl who was expecting around this time of year. Technology didn't allow her to hear the heartbeat, but I'm sure she felt Him kicking...and she knew for sure that she was having a boy. Rocking Him to sleep would have been very similar and since their home was probably very small, checking on Him would have been very easy to do and she knew that, not only would their lives never be the same...all of humanity would never be the same. And what about her prayers for her little Son...I'm sure she figured that He would be a carpenter, just like His dad and there was no doubt that He would be a man after God's own heart. But what about after that...did she know all that was in store for her little Son? Did she realize what He was going to accomplish?

Jewish homes back in those days were the center of life. Girls grew up learning how to make a home and care for a family. Boys learned the trade of their fathers. The Scriptures were taught daily (see Deuteronomy 11:18 &19) and those Scriptures not only included Israel's rich history, but a foretelling of their future. They knew to be expecting a Messiah and they knew that He would have to suffer (see Isaiah 53). Mary would have heard these Scriptures many times and she was told by the angel Gabriel that her child would be called the Son of God, that He would be given the throne of His father David and that He would reign over the house of Jacob forever (see Luke 1).

That's a lot to handle for an expectant mother! Was she able to put the pieces together...did she know that she would have to watch her precious Son die? We're told several times that Mary was a "ponderer"...we may never know all that she was thinking...but I'm sure as she watched Him grow, she was amazed...thinking that it was only yesterday that she held God's Son in her arms...they grow up so fast!

May you have a wonderful Christmas as you ponder Mary's baby and may you realize all He has done for you...and be thankful!

Losing $10

I don't know about you, but every now and then, I find myself making mistakes. Usually, it involves doing something on the spur of the moment, or doing something without taking the time to think it through, or just being careless. It was the latter reason that caused me to make a mistake the other day. I went to Giant Eagle to do my Thanksgiving shopping. Everything that I needed was on sale: turkeys, potatoes, yams, cranberry sauce, whipped cream, pumpkin pie filling, etc. I also had some coupons which made the deals even better! I went through one of those self-checkout lanes and a nice lady from the store saw that I was alone and bagged everything for me. When I was paying, I decided to get an extra $10 out because I didn't have any cash and I wanted to pick up a couple of things at a local little store and thought it would be easier to pay cash there. All in all, a good shopping trip. I stopped at the little store, picked up the items that I needed and got out my wallet to pay...except there wasn't a $10 bill there. At that moment, I realized my mistake...I had left the $10 bill in the change return at the checkout at Giant Eagle. Only 15 minutes had gone by since I left the store and so I called to ask them to set my money aside...but it was gone! Someone had found my $10 and had taken it! I have to be honest, at first, I was really angry at whoever took my money...but then, I found myself asking God to bless them! I realized that maybe they needed it more than I did and I hoped that it helped them to have a better Thanksgiving....or maybe a better Christmas. I also realized that if I'd seen someone along the road holding a sign and asking for help...I would've given it to them anyway! After all, giving is what Thanksgiving and Christmas are all about.

Unfortunately, sometimes we get too busy to remember that. It's so easy to get caught up in all the preparations for Christmas that we don't have time to enjoy and appreciate the season for what it is...a time of giving and joy and wonder and blessings! It's a time when God sent His Son to be our

Savior...not because we deserve it...but because He loves us and wants to bless us as much as we'll let Him.

I know for a fact that whoever took my $10 didn't deserve it...it was mine, but I also know for a fact that, whoever they are, God desires to bless them...and if He used me and my "mistake" to do it...then I was blessed too, because I was used by God to fulfill His will!

May you truly be blessed this Christmas as you give to others and as you receive the greatest gift of all...Jesus Christ...Son of God...our Savior!

Thawing the Freezer

Well, the holiday season is upon us! My shopping is just about done and my baking has begun. I like to get things done early so that I can enjoy the season...reflecting on God's amazing love for us in the peace and quiet of our home rather than battling the crowds in the hustle and bustle of the world!

A few weeks ago, my first seasonal baking consisted of 7 batches of Hawaiian Banana Bread in various shapes and sizes. I chose to begin with this because the bottom shelf of our upright freezer was over-run with over-ripe bananas! When I went to put the freshly-baked bread in the freezer, I realized that our freezer had more problems than just too many bananas. There was too much food in there, some of which had been there too long and the frost build-up was out of control! I decided that the freezer needed a good going-over before my delicious banana bread and the "other baked items to come" could be stored there.

I took everything out, putting the food to keep in a large cooler and throwing the rest away. I turned the freezer off and decided to have some breakfast while I waited for the great thaw! 45 minutes later, it didn't look like anything had happened, so I tried chipping away at it, but that didn't work. I knew I needed help and so I did what any woman would do in this situation...I got my pink blow dryer and got to work! It took a while, but slowly and surely, things started to melt and I was able to break off chunks of ice. Eventually, shiny silver racks began to show through and I marveled at the beauty of those shelves! It had been a while since I'd seen them the way they were made to be and it gave me some peace of mind when the job was all done!

People, at times, can be like that freezer! We have unnecessary baggage that we've been carrying around for far too long and our hearts can become cold and hard. We try to chip away at our problems, but it just doesn't work. We need help. We need the warmth of a loving Savior to melt our cold, hard hearts so that we can, once again, marvel at the beauty of ourselves!

How long has it been since you've seen yourself the way that you were made to be...a beloved child of the King? This Christmas, remember that Jesus came down to earth to be your Savior and let that knowledge warm your hearts and give you peace!

Deadlines!

We face them every day! The kids need to catch the bus on time. We need to get to work on time. Dinner needs to be eaten by a certain time. Products we buy come with expiration dates. We only have "x" amount of shopping days until Christmas and "tax day" is always on April 15th!

Deadlines can be a source of frustration...especially for those who tend to procrastinate...but at least they force us to take action, to accomplish what we need to do...to get the job done! So, in a sense, a deadline can be a good thing...as long as we "take care of business" before we reach that deadline!

Our lives are not only filled with deadlines...they come with one! Unfortunately, we don't know when our "expiration date" is. Most of us spend so much time meeting the small deadlines in life that we ignore the big deadline we all face...procrastinating because we figure we've got plenty of time with no definite date to push us into action!

My intention is not to be morbid, but to encourage us to think about what's really important in life. Yes, I know that it's important to be on time for things and to pay your taxes, but those things are extremely trivial compared to where you will spend eternity!

The fact is, we are all sinners, we are all in need of a Savior and we all have an unknown, yet limited amount of time to "take care of business" before we reach our deadline!

Start the New Year by focusing on what's really important...your relationship with your Heavenly Father. If you've already established that relationship...great! So, focus on building a stronger relationship with Him. Spend some quality time with God, reading His Word and praying. Make attending worship, Sunday school and Bible Study a real priority in your busy schedule!

Strained Muscles & Discipline

A few weeks ago, I strained some muscles in my back and began seeing a physical therapist. In the initial process of evaluating my situation, the issue of my ever-aching knee came up. The physical therapist seemed to feel that he could help my knee. After getting my back straightened around, we began focusing on strengthening my knees and thighs and my knee is feeling so much better.

I have exercises that I'm to do at home and I have to confess that I haven't been doing them daily as I should. I've been blaming that fact on the busy holiday season, when, in fact, it's more a lack of discipline on my part. I know that the exercises are helping me to feel better, so you'd think that I would greet each day with an excitement to do them to improve my quality of life...but other activities always seem to take precedence.

As I'm writing this, I'm reminded of my spiritual life and how when I spend time daily with God, praying and reading His Word, I improve my quality of life. The key is to not let other activities take precedence. Let's all work on that as we begin another New Year!

Driving on Route 136

Driving on Route 136 is like driving on any other two-lane road in Western Pa. You can always count on two things: Lots of curves and slow drivers. The other day, I was traveling down that road and happened to be the "leader of the pack" for a change. Now, I have never been accused of being a slow driver and was, in fact, driving a little over the speed limit. However, the man behind me passed me like I was standing still the first chance he got. Ironically, his haste only caught him up to the driver ahead of me, so all of his hurry gained him about 25 feet!

How many times are we traveling along life's path, jumping at every opportunity to race ahead, only to have God slow us down again? It seems these days that we spend most of our time in a hurry. The typical American family has both parents working and the kids involved in so many activities that sitting down to a family meal consists of riding through the drive-thru of a fast-food restaurant on the way from one practice or game or lesson to another!

In Psalm 46:10 in the Bible, God tells us to "Be still..." so that we can know Him. Now, not only does He want us to take time to pray and read His word so that we can better know Him, He wants us to know Him through our life experiences too.

The family is one of God's blessings and if our families are so involved with their activities that they don't have time to spend with each other, we are missing out on a very special blessing. Here are several examples. Every summer we get to go on vacation and we have always felt that part of the vacation is the trip. Some of our fondest memories were made on the way to our destination. If we are in too big of a hurry to get where we're going, we can miss out on many of God's special blessings along the way. Also, as exciting as it is for an expectant mother to hold her newborn baby, God also gives many blessings during those nine months before: Hearing the heartbeat and feeling the baby kick are memories I'll always cherish.

Let's take a look at our lives and see how we can trim it down so we have the time to be still...and know that he is God!

One of God's Best Ideas

Every year, we compose a Christmas letter to send out to friends as a way of keeping in touch. As we began to think about our letter for this last Christmas, we tried to recall the events of the year, and I said, "Well, let's see. In February, I totaled a car, in March, I turned 40 and in April, I got pregnant! How's that for starters?"

Part of me was joking, but part of me was making a statement about the year not having started out so well! You know that saying about hindsight? Needless to say, my thoughts about last year's beginning have changed – and that's a good thing.

Not so important is the fact that we were able to get a car that's 11 years newer with a lot less miles on it. Next, I was surprised with a wonderful birthday party – a room filled with friends and family from near and far as well as a surprise baby shower later in the year! But, best of all, is the little bundle we received from God on January 8, 1999. Caleb Frederick came into our lives and our lives will never be the same – and that's a good thing.

God, many times, has plans for us that we could never in our wildest dreams imagine and sometimes, as those plans begin to take shape, we question God and His methods. This is where our faith comes in. Sometimes, many times, we fail to see the "big picture", but we need to trust God and know that He only wants what is best for us.

We did a lot of questioning over the last 9 months, but the "5 C's" now know that the "6 C's" was one of God's best ideas. Welcome Caleb! We love you!

Leaving Out the Love

I remember back in the fall when we were trying to teach Caleb to say, "I Love You". We would say "I" and he would repeat "I". Then we would say "Love" and he would repeat "Love". Then, of course, we would say "You" and he would repeat "You". Once he learned the routine, we would say "I" and he would say "I, You". He thought that the goal was to get to the end, but in his haste, he was leaving out the "Love".

How many times in our haste do we leave out the "love?" Remember the little "love" notes you used to write to your spouse when you were dating or that you included in your child's lunchbox when they first started school? Remember when we made time to write letters and make phone calls to loved ones far away? Remember when your Christmas cards used to have personal notes written in each one? We didn't just send them to say hello, but we knew how everyone was doing and what was going on in their lives. Remember when you gave them your undivided attention when they had something to tell you? If it was important to them, it was important to you.

We wonder why we are not as close to people as we used to be. We wonder why our lives are so disjointed. Colossians 3:14 says that we are to "put on love which is the perfect bond of unity". Let's try putting love back into everything we say and do. Let's not be in such a hurry that, like Caleb, we leave out the love.

By the way, the other morning, as I was getting Caleb dressed for the day, I was thinking about all of the things I had to do. Meanwhile, he was calling my name over and over. Finally, I focused on him and what he wanted to tell me. He looked me right in the eye and said, "I love you, Mommy."

Watching People

I love to watch people! I watch them at the mall, at restaurants and at church. I watch them at the grocery store, at craft shows and when I pick Caleb up from school. Children are especially fun to watch...especially when they don't know you're watching.

After school, when I walk up to get Caleb, there's a variety of people waiting to do the same thing. Most of them appear to be parents, but there are also grandparents, aunts, uncles and older siblings...caregivers of all kinds. Many days, I see this one boy in particular. He's maybe in 8th or 9th grade and he gets off his bus just in time to pick up his little brother. While he's waiting, he appears to be very cool... "longish" hair and pants that seem to be two sizes too big and ready to fall down at any moment! He gives the impression that this is the last thing he wants to be doing. As the doors open and the children come down the stairs...their eyes meet...they join hands and I realize that this is exactly what he wants to be doing.

God tells us in 1 Samuel 16:7 that He, unlike man, looks at the heart, not the outward appearance. It's hard not to judge people by what we initially see...but if we take the time, we can eventually see a glimpse of what God sees.

Like I said, I love to watch people...so the other day, "Mr. Baggy Pants" was walking down the hill in front of us and his little brother decided to run. He took off running too...one hand in his brother's and the other holding his pants up! (Go ahead and smile...I did...and I imagine that God did too!)

My name is Cheryl – I'm a mom

The words you are about to read are true; the names haven't been changed because no one is really innocent. "Mom, Carrie wrecked my puzzle!" "Mom, Caitlin won't leave me alone." "Mom, Charlie's being mean to me." If I were Joe Friday, I would've said something like, "Just the facts, kids." But as the Mom in charge, I often said intelligent things like, "Carrie, don't dump the pieces of all the puzzles together!" and "Caitlin, stop touching your sister!" and "Charlie, it's not nice to take the heads off of dolls!" When the kids were small, it wasn't always that they were **doing** things that weren't nice; it was that they were **saying** things that weren't nice too. In those instances, I could be heard to say "If you can't say anything nice...don't say anything at all!

Now I'm not the first Mom to say those words – I'm sure my Mom said them too, along with most other moms. But God was the originator of the idea that we need to watch what we say and how we say it! David so eloquently prayed in Psalm 19 that the words of his mouth and the meditation of his heart be pleasing in God's sight. Paul instructed the Thessalonians to encourage one another and build each other up while reprimanding the Corinthians for their arguing and lack of spiritual maturity. James strongly cautions us that our unguarded words can be like an unguarded flame in a forest. And Jesus warns us in the Sermon on the Mount that with whatever measure we judge or treat others, we will be treated!

From gossiping at work to calling each other names at school to "roast preacher" on Sundays...our words can be very hurtful! We've heard it said that we need to think before we speak, but as Christians, we need to pray before we speak. We need to ask ourselves a few questions like: "Are my words encouraging?" and "Am I building people up with what I say?" and "Is Jesus pleased with my words and actions?" Instead of criticizing everyone from our boss to our teacher to the President of the United States, we should be praying for them!

Jesus wants us to pray for others and to love our neighbors as ourselves. He calls us to a higher standard and expects us to be ever-growing in our faith and reaching new levels of spiritual maturity. He wants us to get along with each other and to be mindful that we are to be witnesses of His love and saving grace.

The kids have matured and have out-grown many of their childish ways. My hope as a mom is that they will continue to mature spiritually as well...as might we all.

My name is Cheryl – I'm a mom.

20/20 Vision

Growing up, I always had 20/20 vision. Chuck, on the other hand, has been wearing glasses since the 2nd grade. One time, after we'd been married for a couple of years, he thought that I should go to an eye doctor for a check-up. So, I indulged him and, after the examination, the doctor told me that if my eye-sight was any better, I could see through walls!

When I was in my late 30's, I worked part-time at a JoAnn Fabrics. One day, I was waiting on an older customer and she was purchasing needle threaders...6 or 7 of them for herself and some of her "quilting" friends. I couldn't understand how someone was unable to thread a needle...and then I turned 43! I first realized that I had a problem when I was having trouble reading my Bible. Then, I noticed that I couldn't read the directions on the back of a medicine bottle. Finally...you guessed it...it took me too many tries to thread a needle!

At first, I wasn't too upset at the prospect of wearing glasses...kids with perfect vision always romanticize the idea of wearing glasses...kind of like wanting a cast on your arm or having to walk with crutches. So, I purchased a pair of reading glasses. I found that I needed them to read the recipe book when making dinner, but not to walk around the kitchen. In fact, I found that walking around with those glasses was an accident waiting to happen! I needed them to see to read my Bible, but not to look up at the preacher or around the table at Bible study...hence, the term "reading glasses". I found myself putting them on and taking them off a lot. I'd take them off in the kitchen and then go downstairs to sew or to do laundry...only to have to go back upstairs to get them. The problem of having to fetch the glasses was easily solved...I bought some other glasses...one for upstairs, one for downstairs and one for my purse. However, the on-again, off-again routine got to be very tiresome and so I, once again, went to the eye doctor and got a pair of prescription glasses... progressive bi-focals with plain glass at the top. I could now leave my glasses on all the time if I wanted to...until a year or so passed and my eye-sight got worse! Considering that the prescription glasses cost me over $200, I opted to go back to the reading glasses.

Then, a new problem arose. We were heading off on vacation in the car one sunny day and I wanted to consult the map...I needed my reading glasses to see the map, but I also needed my sunglasses...so I invented the "double-decker" look, which thrilled my children to no end! I would perch the reading glasses on the end of my nose and then put my sunglasses over top...problem solved...until I forgot to take them off when going into a gas station to buy some water! No wonder they looked at me so funny!

Anyway, I'm still into the reading glasses...one pair upstairs, one downstairs and one in my purse. Occasionally, I find myself grumbling about having to put them on, but mostly, I'm used to the routine...and I am thankful that I have them to wear. I'm also thankful for the many things I *can* see...a beautiful sunrise, colored leaves in the fall, a fresh layer of white snow...my children's faces. I certainly didn't ask for my eye-sight to change...but it has helped me to appreciate things that I used to take for granted. I've also found that my vision has changed in other ways as I've gotten older...I tend to look at people and circumstances through God's eyes (kind of a "double-decker" effect) more than I used to...seeing that He has a purpose for everyone and everything in this life...and seeing the value that He places on you and me...on all of us.

Oh...FYI...last summer I found these reading sunglasses...plain sunglass on top and reading strength sunglass on bottom...very cool!

Pets

Pets! Most of us have them or have had them sometime in our lives. We are going on 37 years of married life and we've only had about a year where we were without any pets!

We currently have two cats...sisters, Jo and Tess. I have a fondness for things pertaining to the old "Wild West" and so Jo is named after St. Joseph, MO (St. Jo for short), home of the famous Pony Express that ran from April 1860 to October 1861. And Tess is named "Tess" because Chuck wouldn't let me name her "Doc" after Doc Holliday, friend to Wyatt Earp!

There are days that they are the sweetest things and days when I wonder what we were thinking when we got them...a little bit like children! ☺ Jo insists on getting on the furniture and Tess likes to play with my decorations...knocking them down and batting them around! She especially likes the artificial pine boughs that I use around the house in the winter. I put a little pick of red berries in them and they look so pretty...until they are all over the floor. I bet I've put one particular pine bough back in its place at least 50 times this season!

I'm sure you're thinking that I should take the easy way out and just put the pine boughs back in their bin in the basement, but I can't do that. First of all, I like the way they look and second of all, there are principles to be considered.

"Whether they be cats or kids", I refuse to let them get the upper hand! (Think like a pirate when you read that line!)

This doesn't seem like much of an "Inspirational Ponderings", but I do have a point, I promise! Sticking to our convictions is important...whether we're talking about naughty cats who play with decorations or children who like to test the waters of disobedience or the foundation of our beliefs! In these days of "Anything Goes" as far as things like faith and morals are concerned, it's essential for us, as Christians, to know what we believe and to stand firm on the sure foundation of Jesus Christ and His Word. When your faith is being tested by the latest idea that society is tossing around, things like abortion, same-sex marriage, co-habitation and sex changes, don't take the easy way out by agreeing with it...stand firm in your Biblical beliefs and trust in the One who provides our sure foundation...God, and God alone!

Being Homesick

I got a phone call this morning from a little girl...well, she's actually 23, but many times, in my eyes, she's still my little girl...telling me that she was homesick! She's a server at the Cheesecake Factory and had several days this week when she didn't have a shift...a usual post-holiday problem with that kind of business...which meant that she'd had several days of being alone. Now, Caitlin has never actually lived in the house where we currently live. Oh, she's been here to visit lots of times, but this house was never actually her home. So, I guess when she says that she's homesick, she doesn't necessarily miss the house, but the people who live in it! You could also say that she misses the "idea" of home...times when she, along with Charlie and Carrie, still lived under our roof. When the kids all make it home in the summer or for the holidays, it seems just like old times, but better, because we can play games and watch movies and talk and laugh without all of the bickering and sibling rivalry that used to take place as well. I guess you could say that our family times are now all of the good, without any of the bad...mostly!

Come to think of it, that sounds a lot like heaven. It's someplace that, as of yet, has never been our home. I mean, we've never lived there, but yet we long for those who are there...loved ones who have gone on before us to live with God...and, God Himself! We like the "idea" of heaven...a place where we can walk and talk with God and each other, but also a place where there will be no more sickness, death or pain...no more tears (Revelation 21:4). Again, all of the good, without any of the bad...completely!

Some people may think it's childish that a 23-year-old would be homesick, but I think it's a good thing. After all, in Matthew 19:14, Jesus said that the kingdom of heaven belongs to the children...or child-like. May we be all be child-like in our faith...with a touch of homesickness for heaven...for home!

Groundhog Day

Back in the early '90's, there was a film called "Groundhog Day" starring Bill Murray & Andie MacDowell. It's about a self-centered TV meteorologist who is forced to travel from Pittsburgh to Punxsutawney, PA to cover the annual Groundhog Day festivities. He grudgingly gives his report and begins to head back to Pittsburgh when a blizzard shuts down all travel and the team is forced to return to Punxsutawney to stay another night.

Phil wakes up to find that he is reliving February 2. The day plays out exactly as it did before, with no one but Phil aware of the time loop. As the phenomenon continues on subsequent days, he goes from being confused to despondent and eventually, inspired by Rita's positivity, he endeavors to improve himself. He begins to use his by-now vast experience of the day to help as many people around town as possible. Eventually, Phil is able to befriend almost everyone he meets during the day, using his experiences to save lives, help townspeople, and to get closer to Rita.

They end up together and Phil is a much better person because of the lessons he's learned along the way and while this movie is by no means a spiritual one, I think there are a few spiritual lessons we can learn.

We may find ourselves in a kind of a spiritual rut, going through the motions of making it to church on Sunday and squeezing a quick devotional in on some days, confessing our sins...vowing never to do it again...and finding ourselves making a very similar confession a few days later. We wonder what's wrong with us...why we keep making the same mistakes, why we can't "be a better Christian", why we never feel like we're making any progress, and why we aren't happier! Does that sound like your life? Well, you may be confused, but before you become despondent, here's a lesson: There's nothing wrong with us or our lives that Jesus can't fix!

Our lives are filled with so much of the same routine...and that isn't necessarily a bad thing...if we make the most of our time spent doing those things. You see, in the movie, Phil had to repeat the same day over and over until he figured things out and got them right, but we don't have to repeat the same day over and over because we have a Savior and He got it right for us and He promises to be with us ALWAYS! He tells us that when we confess our sins to Him, He not only forgives us, but He casts our sins away...as far as the east is from the west! Jesus promises us that each day is new...a fresh start for our life with Him. We do have one thing in common with Phil: it took time for him to straighten his life out and it takes time for us as well. Once we begin our walk with Jesus, we need to spend quality time with Him each day...reading His Word and in prayer...for the rest of our lives...so that our lives will be the best they can be!

So...have a Happy Groundhog Day...and have a life filled with the joy that can only come from spending each new day with a Savior who loves you!

True Love

Love. We misuse it. We misdirect it. We misunderstand it. But occasionally, if we're paying attention, we experience glimpses of what *true love* is. Here are a few of my personal glimpses:

- After having dated for almost two years, I agreed to marry the most handsome boy on campus, knowing that I loved him enough to spend the rest of my life with him. And I thought...surely this is *true love*.
- Four times, following grueling labors and deliveries, I held these red and wrinkled newborn babies in my arms, knowing that I loved them enough to give my life for them. And I thought...surely this is *true love*.
- Standing by the kitchen table, sensing confusion on the part of my aging mother who suffers from dementia, I smiled when I finally heard her call me by name, knowing that I loved this woman who gave me life. And I thought...surely this is *true love*.

These glimpses all have to do with love, but they also have to do with life and that's how we know that we're getting close to what *true love* is. 1 John 3:16 says, "This is how we know what *true love* is: Jesus Christ laid down His life for us." And, the gist of John 3:16 is that out of His love for us, Jesus gave His life so that we might live. I read this and I know...surely this is *true love*!

When we love others with the love of Christ...unselfishly, unconditionally and unrelentingly...we offer them God's gift of life...and that is *true love*!

Saved By Grace!

Every now and then, we have a morning when we don't have anywhere to be. When we have a morning like that, Chuck and I like to have breakfast together and do a crossword puzzle.

Recently, we had the opportunity to do just that, but we also had a little excitement going on outside our house. An oil truck decided to back into the road on the side of our house to bring oil to our neighbor and the driver misjudged the angle and went off the side of the road, knocking down the stop sign and causing the truck to lean precariously toward our neighbor's yard...so much so that the left rear wheel was off the ground.

The passenger got out to assess the situation and he and the driver decided to try to move the vehicle, to no avail. Then, we saw the man on the outside making a call and soon, a huge tow truck arrived at the foot of our driveway. We quickly abandoned our crossword puzzle to watch this live drama!

To make a long story short, these guys were in quite a "pickle" and they needed to be rescued...they needed to be saved! After about 1 ½ hours and trying several different methods, there was success and both trucks were on their way.

We are born into a "pickle": into sin and out of relationship with God. We need to be rescued...we need to be saved, and that can only happen by the grace of God! (Check out the words written on the tow truck!)

A Great Match

Just before Christmas, the Middle School where Charlie and Carrie attend held a Farkleberry Fair. Everyone was asked to donate cookies, which the students could purchase. They also offered a computerized service called "Data Match" where the students would fill out a questionnaire about themselves and then be "paired up" with ten other students from each grade of the opposite sex who share the same interests.

The students had to pay a certain amount in order to participate in this service. All of the money raised during the fair went to Children's Hospital, so the kids had some fun while contributing to a good cause.

After school, as Charlie and Carrie were sharing about the events of the day, we had a good laugh, because Charlie had not only been matched up with ten 8th grade girls, but ten 6th grade girls as well...Carrie being #10 on his list!

As I said, we had a good laugh about this, but as I thought about it, I realized how much sense it made. They *should* have a lot in common: they share the same parents and are being raised to have the same faith and the same set of values and have enjoyed a lifetime of the same family activities.

As we pray for our children, we not only pray that they will grow up living and serving the Lord, but that God will be preparing spouses for them who will also love the Lord. It makes no sense if we pray about our children's future yet neglect to pray about the ones with whom they will share that future.

So, parents and grandparents, pray for your children and set good, faithful examples for them, but also pray that somewhere, some parents and grandparents are doing the same!

Where Has the Time Gone?

Wow! Caleb is seven already! (Or at least he will be this month.) Where has the time gone? Of course, I could say that about a lot of things in life...Charlie's already done with college (didn't we just go to High School Visitation Day?). Carrie's getting married (didn't we just have a wedding between Barbie and Ken?). Caitlin's headed off to college in the fall (wasn't I just late getting home to meet the kindergarten bus?). College was 25 years ago. High School has been almost 30! Our Dads have been gone for more years than we care to remember...

There are a couple of funny things I've discovered about the passing of time: No matter how old you get...you're still you! Over the years, we change physically, mentally, emotionally and spiritually...but inside...I'm still the same little girl who took her clothes off while playing outside on a hot day (We'd better save that for another time!). I'm still the same teenager whose waist-long hair came out of the swim cap in the middle of a meet. I'm still the same young freshman who fell in love with a handsome sophomore at a college dance...and married him!

Time passes by quickly and often we can go a long time without seeing friends and loved ones from our past, but have you noticed that when you see a good friend for the first time in a long time, you can pick up right where you left off?

This month, as Caleb turns seven, I'm reminded of a friend (who also has a birthday this month!). We hardly ever get to see each other, but whenever we talk, it's just like old times. Let me tell you about my friend, Nancy. Nancy was two years ahead of me in college at Grove City. We joined the same sorority and she kind of took me under her wing. We remained friends even after she graduated. She was one of my bridesmaids and I sang at her wedding. We were blessed to live near each other for four years and we picnicked and did the playground thing with our children.

Now let me tell you about something Nancy did...and I will never forget it. Caleb was born in the middle of a snow storm. We lived about 40 minutes from the hospital and after the birth, Chuck needed to get home to the other kids. The next day, there was a state of emergency which meant...no visitors. Nancy lives several blocks from the hospital and didn't she show up that evening...bearing gifts?! I was so happy to have company and so amazed when I found out that she'd walked out in the snow...just to see me! She was still that same college Jr. taking me under her wing!

Proverbs 17:17 says that "A friend loves at all times"...even in a snowstorm...even through the years. Thank you, Nancy...my friend.

P.S. Just so you know, I was only 2 when I had that clothing incident!

Breakfast with a Pirate

This morning, I had breakfast with a pirate! Actually, it was Caleb in all his pirate regalia and I realized, once again, the joy of having a seven-year-old. Sometimes I wonder what our lives would be like if God hadn't given us this surprise baby. Before Caleb was born, Caitlin was the baby and she's headed off to college in the fall, so life would be pretty different!

Do you ever wonder – what your life would be like if it had taken a different path? I do. What if I hadn't gone to Grove City – which is where I met my husband? What if Chuck hadn't decided to be a minister? What if I'd chosen a career over a family? What if I hadn't been introduced to Christ? There are so many decisions to make in life and the different choices we have lead to multiple paths, each having their own set of options. It's mind-boggling!

For the person who feels that life is left up to chance or fate, these decisions, choices and options must truly be a puzzle and, at times, overwhelming. There's a saying that Christians have: "I don't know what the future holds, but I know who holds the future."

As I look back over my life, I see God's hand gently guiding me through all of those decisions. Sure, I've had my doubts and there have been plenty of times when I have felt that I didn't have enough faith to see God's plan for my life. I've had days when I've wondered if I've made the right choices...days filled with dirty diapers or teenage tantrums. But then, my teenage daughter fondly calls me "Mommy" and my seven-year-old lifts up his eye patch and gives me a kiss...and I'm able to share my love for Christ with them and others...and God assures me that I've chosen the right path!

As we celebrate Easter this month, make sure you know the One who holds the future...your future...choose the straight and narrow path...the path that leads to God!

All Things New!

It's the New Year! For some people, this means that it's time to think about losing the weight that you've put on since Thanksgiving...time to change the batteries in the smoke detectors...or maybe buy some new pillows. It's also a good time, as you put away the Christmas decorations, to tidy up the basement or attic...you know, organize all the "stuff" you've accumulated over the years. For some people, the New Year is a time of excitement...of anticipation...of looking forward to the special occasions or vacations that will take place. But for others, it's just a continuation of the same old, same old. Maybe you're stuck in the "same old" job or maybe you're receiving the "same old" unemployment check. Maybe you're experiencing the "same old" life at home that is unfulfilling or full of conflict.

Whether you're trying to structure or trying to scheme or simply trying to survive...remember the lesson of Christmas from the Gospel of Luke: "I bring you good news of great joy that will be for all the people." That proclamation wasn't just made by an angel to some shepherds just for Christmas-time! It was made by God to *all* people for *all* time! It was made for you and for me...for right now...as we start this New Year...whatever our situation. The "good news" is that there is a God and He sees us as we can be yet loves us as we are...with all of our preoccupations...with all of our planning...with all of our pain...and He wants to help us with all of these things so that we can experience the "great joy" that only comes from a life spent with Him!

> I bring you good news of great joy

So, as you begin this New Year...make sure you begin it with God...because according to Revelation 21:5, He is making *all* things new! Blessings for a New Year filled with "great joy".

I'm a Control Freak

I have a confession to make. I'm a bit of a control freak. When I was younger...and had more energy...I rarely wanted anyone's help doing things around the house. No one ever seemed to be able to do it the way I thought it should be done. Now, I ask for help on a regular basis because I've realized that I just can't do it all. However, even when I do accept someone's help, it's hard for me to let them do the job without making little suggestions as to how I would do it! Pathetic! I know! You see, somewhere along the way, I erroneously convinced myself that my way of doing things is the best way and my controlling nature feels that it's my job to get everyone to go along with that way...or else! Also, I have a fear of appearing incompetent or weak...out of control...in front of others. I was talking to someone a few years ago who had a housekeeper come in once a week to clean and I remember thinking, "I'd never want someone coming in to my house seeing how dirty it is...I'd have to clean it up first!" What a silly notion!

You know, that's the way some people feel about God. They like being in control of their lives and they don't think that anyone could do a better job at it...even God. They also don't want God coming in and seeing all the "dirt" in their lives. They think that before they could ever invite God into their lives, they would need to "clean up their act" first! We are only fooling ourselves when we think this way!

God loves us even while we're still sinners (Romans 5:8) and has amazing plans for our lives (Jeremiah 29:11). He wants what's best for us...we just need to trust in Him to make our lives the best they can be (Proverbs 3:5).

I invited God to come into my life a long time ago, and He did, the very moment that I asked, but thirty-some years later, He's still reminding me that He loves me and wants the best for me. He daily encourages me to put my trust in Him and to give Him complete control of my life!

I have a confession to make. I'm a bit of a control freak...but the good news is...I'm better than I used to be...thanks to God and His amazing love for me!

On Being Organized

I received a very unique gift for Christmas. It's a piece of furniture that has 20 drawers in it...perfect to organize my stickers and implements that I use for scrapbooking. I also got a new desk. It's very basic: a 47" top with two shelves on one side. This is to replace the 37" student desk that I've been using. The desk holds my printer/scanner, laptop and mouse pad (which didn't fit on the old desk). The old desk and nightstand that we were using had a total of six drawers between them. Those pieces of furniture are now in the attic and I had quite a job finding a home for everything that was contained in those drawers.

I found a lot of things that had been clipped from magazines. Some were "keepers" and some were not. The many pages on improving your golf stroke and various diets and exercises were not kept, but there were some interesting pages on making memories with your children and other family subjects that I copied and passed on to our children to use with their children.

The best thing I found was an envelope stuffed with little notes that we had received from the kids over the years. Some were thank you notes and some just said "I love you". There were apology notes and proclamations touting us as the "greatest parents ever"! Some were silly or funny and some were very heartfelt. They are all "keepers".

It's a good feeling to start the New Year off being a little more organized, a little bit down-sized. This new furniture helps me to further organize the many on-going projects that I have. I always have a scrapbook project going and I am in the process of scanning all of our old pictures so that I don't have to keep the thousands of hard copies that we have. I am also typing up all of my old "Ponderings" articles from years ago. My working space is so much more "user-friendly" and I know it will be a source of joy to work there during these winter months.

The New Year is also a good time to organize our time with God...finding just that right time of day and a place that is "user-friendly" to spend some time with Him...reading His Word and praying. Some of you may think that time with God should be spontaneous instead of planned...and if that works for you, that's great. I find that if I leave my time with God to "chance", I get so involved in those many on-going projects that, before I know it, the day has slipped away along with my "God time".

Life is very busy with many wonderful things to claim our time. Organize your time enough to make sure that your time spent with God is a priority and a source of joy, peace and comfort! And just like that envelope I found, the Bible is just "stuffed" with all kinds of interesting things, including and most importantly, God's "love notes" to us!

A Family of Notes

I received a note from my granddaughter the other day in the mail. It told of her love for me and that she can't wait to see me. She had drawn little stick figures of herself and me and the page was filled with flowers. She wrote the note on purple paper because she knows that it's my favorite color. That note will go in a special box I have for just such things...once it's done being on my refrigerator door!

I have many other notes in this box. There are love letters from my husband throughout the years and as far back as when he was just my boyfriend; sweet reminders of how much he loves me. There are pages from our kids filled with tender, misspelled words written in crayon expressing everything from their love for us to their penitent hearts when they had misbehaved to their thoughts about God. There's even a letter to the tooth fairy, asking her to take good care of that tooth because it will be missed! There are newsy letters from grandparents, encouraging notes from parents and drawings from other grandchildren as well. Yes, the contents of this box are truly a treasure...ones that I can read over and over again!

I guess we've always been a family of notes. Whenever Chuck would go to a conference, we'd tuck notes in his suitcase for him to find...reminding him of our love for him while we were apart. We would do the same for our kids when they went to camp and I loved putting notes in their lunch bags when I sent them off to school. Every now and then after someone has been home to visit, we'll find a note waiting for us when we go to bed...saying how nice the visit was and how much they love us!

I'm thankful for the letters that I have and I'm hoping to keep receiving them. I'm especially thankful for the letter that God gave us...the Bible. His Word is also truly a treasure...one that we can read over and over again...always learning something new...a reminder of how much He loves us!

The Wild West

I'm a big fan of the Wild West. In the historical novels that I read, my era of choice is any time after the Civil War and before the beginning of the 20th Century. I have a craft room that is decorated with "all things cowboy". I don't think I'd like to live in the late 1800's, but I love reading about that time. Most folks didn't have many possessions, other than what they needed to live, and that included books...but if they did have a book, it was usually the Bible. They also didn't have all of the other distractions that we have today: TV, phones and busy sports schedules.

Somewhere along the way, I came across the "Cowboy Code" and realized how similar it is to the advice we read in the Bible:

1. Live each day with courage.
2. Take pride in your work.
3. Talk less...say more.
4. Always finish what you start.

When Joshua was ready to take the Promised Land, God told him to "be strong and courageous". Paul instructed the Colossians to "work with all your hearts, as working for the Lord". Solomon, in all his wisdom said, "When words are many, sin is not absent, but he who holds his tongue is wise." And lastly, Paul says to Timothy that he has "fought the good fight, finished the race and kept the faith".

Those are some pretty wise cowboys...to get their code from God's Word! May we all follow that code!

Are There Nails in Your Life?

Somewhere along the way, we'd picked up a nail. We limped along, getting air four times, making it to about nine miles from home before the tire finally gave out and we were stranded. That's how we spent our 29th Anniversary. Caitlin's gift to us was a "date-night". She agreed to watch Caleb overnight and we were going to go out to dinner and a movie. We got him delivered to her place and were heading to Olive Garden when someone pulled up next to us on the highway and told us that one of our tires was almost flat! Our new plan was to get home, drop our vehicle off at the garage in town, get our other car and hustle the 45 minutes back to Olive Garden, but that wasn't meant to be. We called AAA and, for some unknown reason, it took the tow truck two hours to get to us! By the time we were able to go somewhere, it was after 9pm and I no longer felt like being anywhere except home!

So, we bought a couple of blizzards and had them for dessert after our dinner of scrambled eggs and toast, watching some movie we owned! If it hadn't been for that nail...things would've been so different! It was not the evening we planned, but it turned out okay...we were safe and we enjoyed some time together alone at home...a rarity, for sure!

Thankfully, we had brought books with us and were able to pass the time reading while waiting for the tow truck to arrive. Unfortunately, I only had about 30 pages to go...so when I was done reading, I began to think. I thought about that nail and how because of it, our plans had changed drastically. Then I thought about His nails...not just one, but three...and how the Disciples' plans had changed. They had left their ordinary, everyday lives and were accompanying Jesus on an amazing journey that was far beyond anything they could have ever imagined. Then there were those nails...forever altering their plans and their lives. They felt stranded. But there was a new plan for them. It wasn't just to watch Jesus perform miracles and preach the Word...it was their turn to do all that...and by the power of the Holy Spirit, they did just that for the rest of their lives.

Are there any nails in your life? Has your life turned out differently than you originally planned? Most of us can answer "yes" to that question. The good news is that God loves us and promises to take care of us if we put our trust in Him! Romans 8:28 says that "God causes all things to work together for good, to those who love God, to those who are called according to His purpose". That means that even when our lives seem like they're a mess, God can take that mess and make it into something beautiful...far better than we could ever imagine...if we trust in Him!

P.S. There's more good news: the wonderful man at the garage was able to salvage the tire and it only cost $10 to have it fixed!

Garden Lessons

The main street that runs through our town is Route 30 (also known as the Lincoln Highway). A couple of years ago, our section of Route 30 got a facelift. The road was re-paved with lines added for parking spaces. The sidewalks were replaced, complete with gradual dips for the driveways and road crossings...making bike riding a breeze! Quaint looking street lamps were added and trees were planted every-so-often in specific places that were left in the sidewalks for that purpose. All in all, a very nice look!

Whenever the weather cooperates, I like to ride my bike to work, using those very nice sidewalks. The other day, when I was doing just that, I noticed that some weeds had popped up through the cement around where the trees were planted. If someone doesn't take up the battle against those weeds, they will soon take over, ruining that very nice look! When I got home, I took a look at our garden, noticing that some weeds had crept into it as well. This summer we planted brussels sprouts, cabbage, cucumbers, lettuce, tomatoes and zucchini. We put up an elaborate fence to keep all of our furry little friends from eating the plants. We used fertilizer to help nourish the plants. We trimmed branches off our tree so that the plants would get the proper amount of sunlight and when there hasn't been enough rain, we water the plants. It takes a lot of work to raise good plants and part of that work is fighting the never-ending battle with the weeds so they don't take over, ruining that very nice garden!

Life is a lot like that. It seems like we have to work hard to cultivate the good qualities while the bad qualities seem to creep up effortlessly into our lives, threatening to take over, filling us with qualities that God detests. In Galatians 5:22-23, Paul mentions some of the good qualities (the fruit of the Spirit) that we, as Christians, are supposed to have: love, joy, peace, patience, kindness, goodness, faithfulness, gentleness & self-control. The Bible also addresses some qualities that we are NOT supposed to have...things like arguing, bitterness, complaining, envy, gossiping & pride, just to name a few. It's not always easy to be patient and full of joy, but it's even harder when we allow things like bitterness and complaining to take up residence in our lives!

This summer, we're going to continue taking care of our garden...nurturing the good plants and removing the weeds as soon as we see them...so that our garden will be a thing of beauty. We also all need to be taking care of our lives...nurturing the good qualities and removing the bad...not only for the summer, but for a lifetime...so that our lives will be a thing of beauty that we can offer to the Lord!

Have a "fruitful" summer!

Kittens & Kids

Getting a kitten last fall wasn't such a crazy thing...getting two was! Bringing these two little fluffy sisters, Jo & Tess into our home seemed like a good idea and we've enjoyed watching them grow over these past few months. However, on occasion, we've questioned our judgment and considered changing their names to Jekyll & Hyde...which would be interchangeable depending on the moment!

Jo will be lying peacefully on the rug in the kitchen (the one that covers the burn mark from the Bible incident last September!) and Tess will be climbing book shelves, knocking things off as she goes so that she can lie down on the mantle amongst the family photos! Moments later, Tess will be basking in the sun on the back of the love seat and Jo will be tearing up the toilet paper! You know how the saying goes, "What one doesn't think of, the other one does!"

I remember feeling this way when the kids were little...having a terrible day where you seriously wondered what you were thinking when you decided to have kids in the first place. And then you check on them before you go to bed and they look so sweet and innocent...and all the nightmares of the day melt away into a peaceful sleep and you wake up the next morning ready to do it all over again!

God does that for us! He knows just what we need...to deal with those "Jekyll & Hyde" situations because He deals with us on a daily basis. One moment we're doing all the right things...and then we're not! But His compassions never fail...they are new every morning! (Lamentations 3:23)

I'm so thankful for the compassion that God has for me and that He gives me for others...and, looking back, I don't regret our decision to have them in our lives...the kids or the kittens!

Stages

As we watched our son approach the stage, his name being called, "Charles Franklin Hildbold, III", my mind flashed to another time, to another stage as he walked up wearing a little white mortar board to receive his Pre-School diploma. He was only 4 years old and had completed his first year of formal education at the Mother Goose Christian Pre-School. This night, 13 years later, the mortar board was green, he was receiving his High School diploma, thus beginning a new chapter in his life.

There have been many "stages" in our son's life. When he was in 1st grade, we got to listen to him narrate the school play on a small stage in East Brady. Throughout the years, we watched our son on the stage called "Home Plate" where he either crossed it in victory or retired his bat in defeat. We've watched him on many stages in various choral concerts, local, county, and state. We've seen him cross the "stage" in 3 different churches as his name was called to receive a perfect attendance pin in Sunday school: 15 years in a row. We've watched many a Christmas Pageant where he's gone from playing an angel to Colby the Computer. He's "wowed" us in 7 different musicals and last summer as he sang with the Continental Singers at our church, following a tour in Europe. Recently, we were able to take the stage with him, as he recited the Boy Scout oath and received his Eagle Scout Award.

Needless to say, we are very proud of Charlie in his accomplishments and the use of his God-given talents. I mentioned earlier that Charlie was beginning a new chapter in his life. This is the time of life when a child formally tests the waters of independence from his parents. This is the time when the proverbial rubber meets the road, when all of the things that a child has learned are put to the test. I'm not referring to his math skills or the history of facts that he's memorized, although those are important. I'm referring to the life lessons he's had; his moral and ethical instruction. I'm referring to the consistent training and upbringing he's had in the Christian faith. Hopefully, just as each of his school years laid a foundation for the next, the training he's had, as a child, will carry him into adulthood.

Proverbs 22:6 says, "Train up a child in the way he should go and when he is old, he will not depart from it." My prayer is that God has been honored by the way that Charlie has been raised and that Charlie will continue to honor God with his life!

We love you, Charlie! Keep the faith!

Grand Canyon!

In June I was able to fulfill a life-long dream: I saw the Grand Canyon! The word "Grand" hardly captures it. In fact, I'm not sure that there are words to describe all that we saw. Our trip encompassed part of what is known as the "Grand Circle". We flew in to Las Vegas and drove to Zion National Park in Utah and then on to Bryce Canyon. From there we went to Page/Lake Powell in Arizona, taking in the Glen Canyon and Antelope Canyon areas. Next, we went to the Grand Canyon and from there to Sedona and Flagstaff. We ended our trip crossing over the Hoover Dam on our way back to Las Vegas. (Fortunately, the traffic was going slowly over the dam and I was able to hop out of the car, put one foot in Arizona and one foot in Nevada, run to catch up with the car and jump back in!)

The lights of Las Vegas are truly a sight and the hotels/casinos are architectural wonders for sure...but they pale in comparison to the majesty of the natural wonders of God that we beheld. If I had to say what we saw in one, short sentence, I would say that "we saw rocks", but the shapes and colors and sheer size of the rocks we saw had us exclaiming over and over: "we are **so** small!" Psalm 8 says, "O Lord, our Lord, how majestic is Your name in all the earth! When I consider the heavens, the work of Your fingers...what is man that You are mindful of him...?"

As we looked at the vastness and beauty of God's creation all around us, we were amazed to think that we are the crown of His creation. What we saw was huge and yet it was only a small portion of all that He has made, and still, He knows each and every one of us...by name...and He loves us!

Staying on Course

Whenever the weather is nice, I like to walk to work. I always have to stop by the post office and it's much easier to stop in when I don't have to find a place to park and get in and out of the car and seatbelt and, of course, it's good exercise. I also like walking because it gives me a chance to read a few pages in whatever book I happen to be reading. A few years ago, they re-did the sidewalks in our town, so they are straight, smooth and even. However, they also put in light posts and some trees that I have to watch out for. I just glance up periodically to make sure that I'm on course...and I always stop reading when I cross the intersection! It makes the walk very enjoyable.

The other day, I kind of got "lost" in a really good part of the book that I was reading and "something" made me look up just before I walked into one of those trees! That not only could have been a catastrophe, but it would have been extremely embarrassing as well!

I prefer to think that it was "Someone" who made me look up rather than "something". I'm not one to believe in coincidence or chance and I don't chalk things up to luck or fate. I don't even tend to "follow my conscience" as much as I follow the leading of the Holy Spirit...some people feel that they are one in the same.

Day by day, as we go about living our lives, it's easy to get "lost" in what we're doing. We need to remember to periodically look up...checking to see that we're on the right course...taking time throughout the day to read God's Word and to spend time with Him in prayer. We should also thank Him for nudging us when we're not paying attention, so that we can avoid an embarrassment, a catastrophe or worse.

If I don't watch where I'm going and get off course when I walk to work, I might run into a tree...possibly getting hurt...definitely being embarrassed...but if I get off course in life...the consequences could be deadly!

Making Plans

I love to make plans. I like to plan my day. I like to plan trips to take. I like to plan meals to prepare. I like to plan Sunday school lessons. I like to plan what Christmas gifts to buy. I like to make plans for the future. I just love to make plans!

For the past three months, my plans have been changed, postponed, canceled...basically dashed on the rocks. All of my calendars (I usually keep up three) have been scribbled and scratched beyond recognition! That's what happens when something unexpected comes into your life, making demands on your time, your days, and your very life! That's what happens when you get sick! Your days suddenly include various appointments and unplanned naps. You can't plan trips because you're not sure what your schedule will be from week to week. Most of the time, meals don't even sound appealing. You're too tired to plan Sunday school, much less teach it. You're just hoping to make it to Christmas and your future seems to be more unknown than it's ever been!

 This is a huge change to be dealing with, and I'm sure that it is downright debilitating to some folks. Thankfully, I don't have to deal with all of this change on my own. I have the support of a terrific husband, a loving family, a caring congregation and prayer partners too numerous to count! I also have the support of the God of the universe who loves me as His child and has given me His Word to encourage and strengthen me.

I have been learning a lot during these past few months. I know that all things are possible with God (Mark 10:27) and that He will give me the strength to make it through this journey (Philippians 4:13). I have learned that if I am still (Psalm 46:10) and if I find my rest in God (Isaiah 30:15), I will know Him and find strength in Him. I know that God is with me (Matthew 28:20), that He will never leave me (Joshua 1:5) and that He helps me in times of trouble (Psalm 46:1). I have learned that He hears my fervent prayers and that they make a difference (James 5:16).

I know that if I put my trust in Him, He will direct my paths (Proverbs 3:5-6) and that He will work all things together for my good because I am His (Romans 8:28). And, I have learned that I don't need to be so concerned about my plans, because God has a plan for my life...a plan to give me hope and a future (Jeremiah 29:11)!

Off to College

I'd forgotten how much is involved in getting someone ready to go off to college...until we started getting Caleb ready.

It all began last year with SAT's and college applications. Now we are knee-deep in financial arrangements, choosing classes and buying books. We've also had appointments with the Dentist, the Eye Doctor and the PCP so that we can turn in all of the necessary medical forms before he goes. We need to go shopping for a list of things that's longer than any list Santa has ever seen and then we have to organize everything...hoping and praying that it will all fit in the car!

Yes, there's a lot to do to get someone ready to go off to college...including preparing your heart for such a huge change!

We hope & dream that they
will make good choices

From the moment our children are born, we begin preparing them for the time when they will leave home...but we forget to prepare ourselves! We're relieved when they are potty-trained and we cheer them on as they learn to tie their shoes. We instill in them a love for reading and we drill them on their multiplication tables and history facts. We hope and dream that they will make good choices and wise decisions and, most of all, that they will have a heart for God...and when our hopes and dreams come true, we aren't always quite sure how to handle it.

You'd think I'd have this down "pat" since Caleb is our fourth child to leave home...yet I find myself struggling. However, he will be leaving in a few weeks, so I've made up my mind to cherish every moment I have with him and to continue to keep him in my daily prayers. I'll be upbeat and excited for him as he embarks on this great adventure. I'll encourage and support him as he discerns God's plan for his life.

In private, I'll shed a few tears as I prepare to miss this child of mine who has grown up so quickly...but I'll thank God for the young man that he has become and I will depend on God's love and comfort as I embark on this great adventure as well!

Collecting Sea Shells

Well, we just finished our annual week at the beach. We had a good week: good to get away...good to get back home. However, the thought of living there did cross my mind...

As I look back on the week and all of the fun things we did...one of my favorite times was when Caitlin and I walked along the shore collecting sea shells and pretty stones. The feeling of her small hand in mine; the wonderment as she discovered various treasures for her bucket; the words, "I love you, Mommy" as we completed our journey...

I didn't bring home any spectacular shells or win any grand prizes at the games but I did bring home a treasure: the memory of these moments shared with one who is growing up very fast...moments never to be recaptured.

Caitlin did bring home some shells (more than her Dad wanted her to) as well as a prize from a game and, for now, they are her treasures. But some day, when those shells are long gone, when the thrill of the game is forgotten, I suspect she'll still remember that walk in the sand with her Mom and her treasure will no longer be in her hand but in her heart. Then she can say along with the apostle Paul, "I thank my God every time I remember you"...Philippians 1:3.

Take time this summer to make some memories, to share some unrepeatable moments with someone you love. Do something worth remembering and discover one of God's greatest treasures.

White Board Words

Recently, Chuck and I spent a few days in New Jersey with our daughter, Carrie and her family. Our grandchildren were excited to see us when we arrived, but I didn't realize how much they were looking forward to our visit until I saw a weekly white board with these **words**:

- Monday: get ready for Nana and Papa
- Tuesday: get ready for Nana and Papa
- Wednesday: Hump Day!
- Thursday: Nana and Papa are coming ☺
- Friday: Beach time (with Nana and Papa)
- Saturday: Nana and Papa are leaving ☹

I can't tell you how loved their **words** made us feel!

Words are very powerful and the Bible has a lot to say about them. In the Psalms we read that God's **Word** is flawless and a light to our paths. In the book of Proverbs, we read that a kind **word** cheers, but a harsh **word** stirs up anger. In the Gospel of John, we read that Jesus is the **Word** and that by Him, all of creation was spoken into existence and in Paul's first letter to the Thessalonians we read that our **words** should be used for encouraging each other and building each other up.

I have tried to make it a habit lately to compliment people: I tell them that their clothes or hair are pretty or that they have a nice smile or that their children are cute...anything to encourage them. Just as our grandchildren's **words** made us feel loved, I want my **words** to make others feel loved and for them to know that this love comes from God!

I Miss the Kids!

I miss the kids when they're at school. I think about them during the day...wondering what they're doing and how things are going for them. It seems as though they're gone for such a long time and when they are home, we're either busy getting ready for school or getting ready for bed so that they can go to school the next day.

Oh sure, there's some homework and studying for tests sandwiched in between with little time left for anything else! However, we make it through...taking one day at a time and looking forward to holidays and the days off they have scattered throughout the year. The big countdown comes though, as summer vacation approaches! Each day we check in with each other to make sure we've got the right number. "Only 12 more mornings to get up early." "Only 11 more nights to go to bed early." "Only 10 more evenings of homework!" I don't know who's more excited...the kids or Mom! This is really a time to celebrate!

Summer vacation! Trees newly leafed out in all of their splendor, flowers, the smell of freshly-cut grass, even the bees are a sign that summer is nearing. We're busy making plans for trips we'll be taking, friends and relatives we'll be visiting and movies we'll be taking in at the local drive-in. We're dreaming about all of the swimming and camping and biking and skating and swinging and baseball games. Summer is truly a time to celebrate!

However, summer is also a time to be careful. With all of the wonderful things being planned for our summer celebration, let's not forget to include God in our plans. He's the One who made the trees and flowers. He's the One who gave us wonderful families to enjoy!

As you share this special summer time with your kids, making a lifetime of memories, be careful to include God in your celebrating. Have family devotions around that campfire or on the beach as you watch the first star of evening appear.

Make sure that you go to church...wherever you are this summer. Make sure that God is a part of the celebration! Have a great summer!

Who is This Guy, Anyway?

As I write this, I'm thinking about my life, as it was 20 years ago. On Saturday, May 17, 1980, I graduated from Grove City College. I'm so thankful that God led me to a school where I could work on my education and build relationships that would last a lifetime. One of those relationships is what I'd like to focus on this month.

My very first class in college was called "Life of Christ". Once we were all seated, the professor welcomed the incoming freshmen and then asked the returning sophomores to tell about their summers. One young man started sharing about his summer and used up most or all of the time allotted for that discussion. I remember turning to a fellow freshman saying, "Who *is* this guy, anyway?"

A great thing about college is that in addition to your classes, there are many activities from which to choose as well. That first week of school, I had heard about a singing group called "Gospel Team" and decided to check it out. Their meetings/rehearsals were held in the chapel and as I walked down that long aisle toward the front, who did I see…that guy from my "Life of Christ" class…sitting at the piano…and I was introduced to Chuck Hildbold. Funny how God works! It wasn't until my second semester that we started dating and we built our relationship over the next three years.

We hit it off right away because we had a lot in common: a love for the Lord and a love for music, to name a couple. God uses similarities to draw two people together, but He uses the differences to help them complement each other.

Recently, in Sunday school, we were discussing God's old covenant with the Israelites and His new covenant through Jesus Christ. We noted how Jesus claimed to be fulfilling the old covenant, not replacing it. That's how a marriage ought to be. Each person brings their unique individuality to the relationship, but it's the uniting of the two that completes them.

As Christ loves the Church, so a husband should love his wife. Sounds like something said at a wedding, doesn't it? Remember when I graduated? Well, three weeks later, on June 7, 1980, I walked down that long aisle of the chapel at Grove City College and God introduced me to my husband, Chuck Hildbold.

Happy 20th Anniversary, Chuck. I love you.

It's My Choice

Our house is on a beautiful, tree-lined street. The trees are large and provide shade. However, this time of year, as the new leaves are coming to full size, the trees are also losing their seeds. Daily, hundreds, maybe thousands of little "helicopters" float down to cover the grass, the mulch, the sidewalks, the steps, the gutters and our front porch. We have a great big front porch with an awning for shade and a painted wooden floor. I love spending time out there but can only enjoy it when it's clean. So, several times a day, I'm out on the porch sweeping it off.

It's tempting to wait until the seeds are done falling and do the job once and for all instead of so many times, but isn't that how life is? When I stop to think about it, most of what I spend my time doing involves things that have to be done over and over again. Making beds, running the sweeper, dusting, cooking, laundry, shopping...the list goes on and on. If I were to focus on that too long, I could get depressed about how I spend my life...kind of like spinning your wheels.

Something else I've been doing this spring is catching up on our photo albums. I was two years behind, which is a lot for me. In the process, I've been looking at many of the pictures over the years and have been reminded of the many memories we've shared as a family. College days, a beautiful wedding, four births, first steps, getting the training wheels off the bikes, snow forts, leaf piles, game nights, wrestling with Daddy, sand castles at the beach, gorges in New York, waterfalls in Maryland, prayers said by the bed at night...and the list goes on and on.

It's my choice...I can focus on the mundane chores of life or I can focus on the many blessings that the Lord has given us over the years. We have a promise in Jeremiah 29:11, "For I know the plans I have for you declares the Lord, plans to prosper you and not to harm you, plans to give you hope and a future." I choose the memories...those from the past and those we've yet to experience.

Caleb & T-Ball

Watching one of Caleb's Tee-Ball games is a bit like watching a 3-Ring Circus. You're never quite sure where to look because there's something going on all over the field. There's the kid on 2nd base who's looking at the world upside down from between his legs and the girl who's watching the pretty butterfly go by. The "pitcher" wears a protective helmet and the other day, the boy had it pulled down over his eyes and had his head in the dirt! Caleb can usually be seen spinning around in place for some reason. And the batters all take several wind-ups before hitting the ball...off a tee!

What do we expect? They're still learning the game. There are rules that they need to know in order to play. They need to learn about strikes and foul balls. They need to learn about tagging the bases and sliding. They need to learn about catching and throwing. In addition to the rules, they need to learn about things like good sportsmanship and fair play. Oh, and something we're ALWAYS telling the kids...keep your eye on the ball!

It's the same with their spiritual lives (and ours, for that matter!). They need to learn about the faith of Abraham and the courage of David. They need to learn about the persistence of Joseph and the obedience of Moses. They need to learn about not stealing and lying and about honoring your parents. But, in addition to the history and rules, they need to learn about having a personal relationship with Jesus Christ. Oh, and throughout their lives, we need to keep telling them...keep your eyes on the Lord!

"Stealing" the Tube

We have checking accounts at two different banks: one in town that we use all the time and one that's about five miles away that we use periodically. One day, I had a few errands to run that included a trip out to that "periodic" bank as well as to the grocery store. I decided to go to the bank first and seeing that there was no line at the drive-up window, made that my choice for making my deposit. Now the bank in town only has one window...you drive up and a little drawer comes out, you put your banking items in there...well, you get the picture. On the other hand, the out-of-town bank has two places where you can do your banking from your car and they have those capsules that you put your banking items in and then you push a button and the capsule goes shooting up a tube and into the bank...much more exciting! Anyway, I had just completed that process, when my cell phone rang. It was my sister and since we hadn't talked in a while, we had a lot of things to talk about. Before I knew it, my capsule came back down the tube and the teller inside thanked me and I was off to the store. In Pennsylvania, we're still allowed to talk on the phone and drive at the same time, and so my sister and I talked the whole five miles to the store. However, I do not get reception on my phone in the grocery store, so when I arrived at the store, I told her that I needed to go. I went to put my phone back in my purse, and that's when I realized...I'd kept the capsule! Needless to say, I did my shopping very quickly and then headed the five miles back to the bank, where I walked in holding the capsule and the nice teller said, "So, that's where it went!"

I wanted to share this story with you for one purpose and one purpose only: so you could laugh! Sometimes we take life, in general, and ourselves, in particular, way too seriously. Now, don't get me wrong, there are things in life that must be taken seriously...things like managing your finances, keeping your marriage vows and living out your faith. But when we do something silly, it's good to admit it and to learn from it and definitely to laugh about it! Solomon said in Proverbs 17:22, "A cheerful heart is good medicine, but a crushed spirit dries up the bones." Do you have any ailments? Try following God's prescription: watch a funny movie, read a funny book, have a good laugh with your friends...make your heart cheerful!

Just in case you need another laugh...ask me about the time I went through the automatic car wash...and didn't get on the track! Only one side of the car got clean and I almost hit the lady in front of me!

I Hate Dust!

I hate dust! I know I'm not supposed to say "hate" (one of our family rules), but I think that it's okay to hate something like dust. I can dust in the morning and by afternoon, the dust is back...forming its evil layer over the surface of our furniture! Of course, the dust shows more readily on some pieces of furniture than on others. Take our piano, for instance...it's made of a dark wood with a high sheen which, when given the proper care, reflects its surroundings. It's located right next to the main thoroughfare of our living room and is forever plagued by dust and fingerprints! The piano is the first piece of furniture to let me know that it's time to eradicate the dust. On the other hand, our entertainment center is made of light wood and does a pretty good job of hiding the dust. However, on a nice day when the sunlight streams in through the windows, all of the dust is brought to light and I am discouraged and ashamed at the state of my house.

You know something else I hate? I hate sin! I can repent of a sin in the morning and by afternoon, sin is back...infiltrating its evil into my life! If I could be like any piece of furniture in our house, I would choose to be like the piano...quick to know when sin needs to be dealt with and reflecting the Father's love...not to mention having the capacity to make beautiful music! Unfortunately, I am more often like the entertainment center...filled with things that are of no eternal value and able to hide my sin for a season...until the "Sonlight" shines into my life, exposing my sin for all to see...leaving me discouraged and ashamed at the state of my life.

When the state of your furniture is what brings you discouragement and shame...dust it! When it's your life...give it over to God! In John, chapter 8, Jesus said that He is the Light of the world. So, let His light shine on your life, exposing all of your sin and let Him cleanse you, wiping away all of the discouragement and shame, so that you can be a reflection of His love to everyone you meet on the thoroughfare of life!

Joy in the Journey

I love to scrapbook and I am currently working on one about our travels, and as wonderful as the destinations have been, I've discovered that there is also much joy in the journey!

I have a lot of pictures of the places we've visited and some wonderful memories of those places as well, but some of my fondest memories are of the moments that took place on the way to where we were going:

- Driving slowly when approaching a red light...keeping the car in motion so the kids would stay asleep...holding onto those precious & few moments of peace and quiet...and don't tell me you parents don't know what I'm talking about!

- 3 kids crowded in the backseat...blanket barricades in between them!

- Playing the "Alphabet Game" and "I Spy"...again!

- Keeping track of how many different license plates we see!

- Charlie leaning forward just enough so he could hear what we were talking about without us knowing...ha!

- Taking turns picking out what CD to listen to!

- Driving through Utah and being "wowed" by the scenery that we saw at every turn!

Remembering all the journeys we've had is wonderful...but I also love to think about our journey as a whole. When I began this scrapbook, I decided to start with our honeymoon to the Outer Banks of North Carolina...the first trip we took together. This month, we are going back to the Outer Banks to celebrate our 30th Anniversary and 30 years in the ministry...just one more step in the wonderful journey that God has called us to take together.

As Christians, our final destination is Heaven, but God also gives us this amazing journey along the way... "wowing" us at every turn...surprising us with memories that we'll never forget...and, through it all...loving us! I'm thankful that my journey has been with God and also with the wonderful man that He gave me! Happy Anniversary, Chuck! Thanks for the journey...so far...and thanks for loving me along the way!

"I am stuck on band-aid, 'cause band-aid's stuck on me..."

Most of us are familiar with this little jingle, written by Barry Manilow. It's been around since the 70's and is still going strong through generations of kids with "boo-boos"! Some of the lyrics have changed over the years, heralding the little miracle-workers that stay on in "soapy suds" and on "fingers, toes and knees" ...protecting us from "germs" and "healing our hurts" ...but the tune and the chorus have stayed the same... "I am stuck on band-aid, 'cause band-aid's stuck on me!"

I am bringing this up not just for nostalgic reasons, but because I know of a little band-aid that has proven the jingle to be true...and because there's a lesson to be learned!

Last July (eleven months ago), as I was taking my usual brisk morning walk, I noticed a band-aid on the road. I didn't think much of it...until I saw it there the next day and the day after that. I began watching for the band-aid and eventually began expecting to see it. It remained there all through the long hot summer and into the fall. As winter came and brought its snow and ice, I thought for sure that the little band-aid would lose its sticky-ness and be scooped up by the snow plow. When Spring came and I began to walk outside again...I was surprised to see that the little band-aid was still there! That little band-aid has been scorched, frozen, soaked and run over...yet there it remains...a symbol of strength and perseverance!

Life can throw a lot at us! We may feel like we've been scorched by a dis-loyal friend, frozen by a love-less marriage, soaked by a thank-less boss and just plain run over by the whole world...but we need to remember that we have a "friend who sticks closer than a brother" (Proverbs 18:24)...someone who stands by us under all sorts of conditions...protecting us and healing our hurts...and that someone is Jesus!

❀ 99 ❀

So, when you're facing life's "boo-boos", remember that you are God's precious child and sing an old song with some new lyrics: "I am stuck on Jesus, 'cause Jesus' stuck on me"!

Surgery

I recently had arthroscopic knee surgery to repair a torn meniscus and my "road to recovery" has included some physical therapy. I have 12 exercises that I do daily which serve two main purposes: to build up strength and to increase mobility. The mobility exercises have to do with my knee, but the strengthening exercises have to do with my thigh. You see, the knee is controlled by the thigh...so to have strong knees, you have to have strong thighs! During my last session, I asked the Physical Therapist how long I should do these exercises and I was told that I could do them for the rest of my life...that they would always be good for me!

The Bible has a lot to say about strength...and it always has to do with God! God promised to be with Moses and give him the strength to free the Israelites from their Egyptian slavery. Joshua and Caleb knew that God would give them the strength needed to conquer the Promised Land. David's strength was in the Lord as he felled the 9-foot-tall Goliath. Daniel trusted God's strength to shut the mouths of the lions. Nehemiah knew that the joy of the Lord was his strength and Paul knew that he could do all things through Christ who gives him strength!

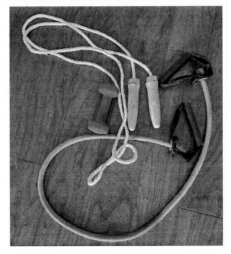

Becoming a believer in Christ is a little like undergoing surgery...realizing that something needs to be repaired in our life and taking care of it by asking Christ into our heart. Our "road to recovery" includes some spiritual therapy...some exercises to do daily so that our faith is strengthened and increased. Read God's Word and spend time in prayer...discover what so many of our Bible heroes knew:

that God is our source of joy and our source of strength and that with Him, we can conquer anything that comes our way!

I have found through this experience how much I really want to be able to walk and ride my bike...and get down on my knees...and so I will continue to do my daily exercises in order to strengthen my legs, giving me the best quality of life possible. And I will also continue to my daily spiritual exercises, giving me the best life here...and in eternity!

Titles!!

We are all associated with a variety of them. From the moment I was born, I instantly and automatically held the title of daughter and little sister...by no choice of my own. In my teens, I felt the call of God on my life and chose to accept His gift of salvation through His Son, Jesus Christ, thus receiving the title of a daughter of the King! When I was in my 20's, I chose the title of wife and eventually, mother. When I was 50 years old, I got a phone call from our daughter, Carrie telling me that she was bestowing another title on me...grandmother...not my choice...I didn't feel that I was old enough to have that title!

Now, at 58, I am a grandmother five times over and my title is "Nana". I don't live right next door to any of my grandchildren, but we see each other periodically throughout the year...and they are all a delight!

As a Nana, I get to read the stories that I read to our kids like "Horton Hears a Who", "Make Way for Ducklings" and "Are You My Mother?" I get to color and build castles with the old wooden blocks that were mine as a child. I am the recipient of colored scribblings and messages of love which I proudly display on my refrigerator. I've seen a video of Gracie calling me on her toy phone, telling me how much I am loved and missed. I recently received a beautiful bouquet of purple wildflowers, hand-picked by Emily and Daniel because they know that purple is my favorite color and Emily included me in her lunch-time prayer the other day.

I get to shop for toys again and make homemade cards for our grandchildren to put in their keepsake boxes. I get to teach them about Jesus and of God's love for them. I can crawl after Micah, relishing as he squeals with delight in the chase and Jude is still little enough to cuddle. I get to watch amazedly as these little children run into my open arms, giving me hugs and kisses and saying, "I love you, Nana."

Whether they were by choice or not, all of these relationships have been such a blessing to my life and have helped to shape me into the person that I am. God has had a plan for my life from the beginning and it is amazing to look back over how He has orchestrated all of the choices that I thought were mine and aligned them with His good and perfect will for my life. I am both proud of and thankful for all of the titles that are mine!

Goals

G oals are, for the most part, a good thing to have. There are always goals in sports. In baseball, you want to get a hit, hopefully cross home plate to score a run and ultimately win the game for the team. In football, the goal is to score a touchdown and ultimately win the game for the team. In swimming, your goal is to beat your last time and beat the time of the other swimmers...and, of course, ultimately win the meet for the team. Personally, my goal for each day is to get 10,000 steps in. (Sometimes, at the end of the day, I've been known to read my book while walking around the house so I can reach my goal!)

I have a smart phone and I can do many, many things on this phone, including playing games. One of my favorite games to play is Free Cell Solitaire. When I first discovered this game, I would just play a game here and there, just to play. But then I realized that there were daily goals set for you and they are different each day. Having these goals makes the game more interesting because I'm not just playing, but I am striving to reach the set goals.

Having goals makes life more interesting too. Goals encourage us to work harder, to do better, and to stretch ourselves so that we can become a better person.

Having goals in our Christian walk does the same for our spiritual growth. They encourage us to stretch ourselves so that we can become the person that God wants us to be.

Goals encourage us

Here are some goals that would be good for Christians to set for themselves:

- Attend worship as often as you are able. Make it a priority.

- Be part of a small group: a community group, a Sunday school class, or a Bible Study.
- Set aside some time each day to study God's Word on your own, a time of personal devotions and to spend time in prayer.
- Find times when you can "be still...to know that He is God".
- Pray about and look for opportunities to witness and minister to others with acts of service.

When we set goals and strive to meet them, we have a renewed sense of purpose. When we succeed in meeting them, we have a renewed sense of accomplishment.

When we set goals for our Christian walk and meet them...we have a renewed relationship with God!

When we experience spiritual growth, we have more to contribute to the body of Christ in our church, our community and around the world...and that's winning one for the team!

The Best Marriage

Recently, the local Christian radio station had a contest for Valentine's Day. Women were to write marriage proposals to their husbands, proclaiming their love for them and asking them to marry them all over again. I didn't think much about the contest until I heard what the finalists had to say. Now don't get me wrong, their proposals were fine, but I thought that I could do better. No, it's not Valentine's Day nor is it our anniversary, but we did kiss for the first time 27 years ago this month! With that in mind...here goes!

Dear Chuck,

I love it when you make my tea.

I love it when you rub my back.

I love listening to music with you.

I love making music with you.

I love watching movies together and that you don't laugh at me when they make me cry.

I love it when we go out to dinner or go to a play or to a baseball game...I'd go anywhere with you.

I love waking up to your face and I love being lulled to sleep by the rhythmic sound of your breathing.

I love it that we had four children together and that you've always been there to share that joy & responsibility: from diapers to driving lessons to diplomas, you've always been there.

Most of all, I love it that you're a man after God's own heart.

God's Word tells us in 1 Corinthians that "love is patient, love is kind. It does not envy, it does not boast, it is not proud. It is not rude, it is not self-seeking, it is not easily angered, it keeps no record of wrong. Love does not delight in evil but rejoices with the truth. It always protects, always trusts, always hopes, always perseveres. Love never fails."

I love it that I found that kind of love in you.

I can't imagine life without you.

I'm so glad that God brought us together all those years ago and I want you to know that I'd love to marry you all over again!

  Well, I did it! At first, I wondered if it was appropriate to put such a writing in the Church newsletter, but then I remembered that marriage is a covenant instituted and ordained by God. And I thought that He would be pleased.

Carrie, China and Crystal

Our daughter, Carrie, will be turning 16 in June. Now when you think of someone turning 16, two definite things come to mind: getting a license and getting a job. Carrie, being the second-born in the family, (I'm a firm believer in the effects of birth order!) is not terribly interested in either prospect. She's not afraid of driving or working; she's just not in a hurry. And that's okay! However, when you look at the situation from our perspective, we have a licensed son who will be leaving for college in the fall. Also, Carrie has a boyfriend who lives in a different area code, which leads to phone bills of a larger amount than any allowance can handle!

Let me address the driving issue first. Those of you who have older children know how it is when your first child gets his or her license. At first, you're very apprehensive to let them go anywhere, but little by little, you get more comfortable with the idea. Before you know it, you're saying, "Charlie, would you please run to the store and get some milk?" "Charlie, would you please go pick your sister up from school?" "Charlie, the van needs gas, would you mind?" Suddenly, you realize how nice it is to have a "gopher", I mean an additional driver who is not only capable, but also willing! They're happy for any chance to drive and we're happy not to have to run all those errands. It's basically a win/win situation. THEN COMES COLLEGE and just like that, we lose our "gopher", I mean our highly capable third driver! Here's where Carrie comes in. Of course, we would never push her into doing something about which she is uncomfortable, but we also will encourage her in the direction we feel she needs to go...after all, we had our children 2 years apart for a reason, right?

Now, let's talk about this job thing. The other day, I was trying to think of job possibilities in the area: fast food, grocery stores and HALLMARK. Now that, I thought, sounds like a nice place for a young lady to work. And then I remembered the ONLY time I took Carrie into a Hallmark store. Picture this: she's 5 and Caitlin is 2 and we're in a very small mall where there's a K-Mart with shopping carts. That day, I had forgotten the stroller and had to use a cart to make my way around the mall. Caitlin is riding, Carrie is walking and I'm browsing in Hallmark. Now remember, Hallmark doesn't just carry cards. They have photo albums and stuffed animals and GLASS shelves with BREAKABLE trinkets on them. Needless to say, while I was browsing, the girls decided to have one of those unpleasant sibling moments and Carrie gave the cart a shove right into one of those glass shelves. Fortunately, I was only out $10 (it could've been $100!) and I vowed never to take Carrie into a store like that again! Wouldn't it be just like God for her to get a job in there? The God who forgives and forgets all of our past mistakes and puts us right into a situation that tests our faith and makes us strong!

Well, I'm *not* sure what will come of this "turning 16" thing! I do know that Carrie is now taking driver's theory at school and that Charlie's boss at Subway has told her to come in and fill out an application. I *am* sure that God will work all things out in His own timing.

One more thing for you to picture: it's raining and you're going to the Westmoreland Mall. You park under cover and enter the mall through Kaufman's. You make your way through the store to get to the rest of the mall and what do you have to walk past...CHINA AND CRYSTAL!!! It's a good thing that God forgets our past mistakes, because it's hard for us parents to!

Be Careful Little Ears...

Call me naïve, but it never ceases to amaze me how people can lack the morals I believe to be basic to all human beings. Many societies and cultures, not just Christians, feel that it is wrong to use vulgar language or curse and to lie, but I found myself in the midst of two such instances a few weeks ago.

One day, I needed to go to the grocery store, but since the weather was bad, I decided to wait until the kids were home from school to watch Caleb so that I didn't have to take him out in it. I was heading toward the bananas, following a man with a 2–3-year-old in his cart. As we reached our destination, he saw someone he obviously hadn't seen in a long time. She began to swear using every word imaginable to describe just how long it had been. I expected the man to tell her not to use such language around his impressionable toddler, but he merely laughed and joined right in! I can only imagine how this child will talk as he grows up!

Speaking of bad weather, most of you are aware that I've been delivering Carrie's newspapers for the winter and lately have had to walk through a lot of snow. Some people shovel their sidewalks and stairs and some don't. One day, I was heading for a set of treacherous stairs, which obviously hadn't been shoveled since the first big snow the week before. I know because I'd gone up them every day. On that particular day, a lady pulled up to the curb with her Middle School-aged son and I said how nice that she had a son who was old enough to shovel. She proceeded to tell me that he'd just done the steps the day before. Now, I knew that this wasn't the case and I expected the son to say something like, "No I didn't, Mom.", but he went right along with her story. My guess is that he is so accustomed to her lies, they no longer strike the chord in him that tells him when something's wrong. How sad!

Mark 9:42 says: "If anyone causes one of these little ones who believe in me to sin, it would be better for him to be thrown into the sea with a large millstone tied around his (or her) neck." A few verses later we read, "Let the little children come to Me, and do not hinder them, for the kingdom of God belongs to such as these."

Parents. Be careful not to lead your children astray. These little blessings are entrusted to us and their lives and our future depend on the example we set. Let it be a good one!

Lost Ground

How many of you like to exercise? Well, let me put that another way...how many of you recognize the need for it and, therefore, perform some sort of exercise? I actually like to exercise...most of the time. I like to walk on the treadmill or on the Boardwalk when we're at the beach. I also like to use a mat up in my room in order to do some stretches and "ab" exercises. I especially like to do these in the morning which isn't always easy because I'm usually busy doing some sort of juggling act at that time of day. But I try to make it a priority because it's important, I enjoy it and the more days you miss, the more ground you lose! You know what I mean...you finally get into a good routine...you notice that it's becoming a little easier, so you have to increase your activity...life gets busy and you take a few days (or weeks) off...you're back to square one. You have to start all over again and that can be discouraging and even painful because those muscles have gotten lazy!

I know this from experience because back in November, I could hardly walk. To make a long story short, I had a stress fracture on my right foot and had to take 2 months off from the treadmill in order to allow my foot to heal. It was tough getting back in the "groove"...I had to take "baby steps" and am still building back up to where I was last Fall. Unfortunately, with exercise, you can't just pick up where you left off...and isn't that the way it is with a lot of things in life? Many times, we'll run into an old friend and the ease of our conversation leads us to believe just that...that we picked up right where we left off. No, we didn't! There's been a lot of life going on since we last saw each other and even if we had the time to "catch up", we'd still have some lost ground in there that we'll never regain.

When Charlie, Carrie and Caitlin were young, we had quite an ambitious Scripture memory program at our house. So, when Caleb was old enough, we "re-instated" the program. He was doing well and then we got lazy or busy and stopped working on them until just recently. He lost ground. It'd been long enough that we had to start all over again! And what about our walk with God? We finally get into a good routine...we participate in many spiritual growth opportunities at our church...we never miss a day of our quiet time...then life gets busy and we take some time off...

Set-backs can be discouraging. Building our faith can be difficult...but you know what they say about things that are worthwhile! When we've lost ground in some area of our life, the important thing to remember is to move ahead. Paul gives us some good advice in Philippians: "Forgetting what is behind and straining toward what is ahead, I press on toward the goal to win the prize...". The prize can be finding and sticking with an exercise program that works for you...keeping in touch with your friends so you don't have so much "catching up" to do...and most importantly, making your walk with God a priority in your life!

Got some "lost ground" in your life? Forget about it and move on toward the life that God has planned for you.

Remodeling

We are in the middle of remodeling the kitchen...new cupboards, new sink, new countertop and new wallpaper. We have professionals doing most of the work, but we were elected to remove the old wallpaper. The wallpaper we had was country blue and pink on a white background...typical of the late '80's / early '90's. Underneath were remnants of the previous style...brown and white checkered with "kitcheny" pictures in gold, orange and avocado...typical of the late '60's / early '70's. Beneath it all was the famous industrial green...somewhere between a mint and a turquoise, which brought back vivid memories of elementary school!

There are some places on the wall where the paper comes off easily and other places where we really have to scrape to get it off. This is an old house

"God is the glue in all of this"

and so obviously, this is not the original wallpaper. There are several layers of paper and paint...and glue! It's interesting to see the different layers, each representing a particular moment in time. It's also interesting to think of all the memories that these walls were privy to...all the meals shared, all the conversations spoken, all the prayers prayed, all the cooks kissed, all the laughter, all the tears, all the life!

Our lives are a lot like these walls...lots of layers, each representing a particular moment in time. Take my life, for instance. The current layer shows a woman who's experiencing a combination of the empty nest and reliving PTO and Cub Scouts! Peel back a layer and she's rocking her babies to sleep while singing "Turn Your Eyes Upon Jesus". The next layer down is of a young woman in college, meeting the man of her dreams and before that is a girl who's searching for something that's missing in her life...God. God is the glue in all of this. God is what holds all of our layers together! God has been privy to my whole life...the conversations spoken, the prayers prayed, the kisses in the kitchen, the laughter, the tears...all of it!

Stripping away layers of wallpaper isn't always the easiest thing to do, but it's necessary and in the end, it's interesting and rewarding. Examining the layers of our lives can be difficult too, but it's necessary if we're going to understand what God has been doing in our lives and discover the plans that He has for us in the future. (See Jeremiah 29:11).

Speaking of the future, I have no idea what kind of wallpaper we're going to be putting on the walls next, but we can make sure that we create a lot of wonderful memories for the walls to enjoy!

Be Careful Little Eyes

It was a chilly day. The house was cool and the wind outside was howling. I spent a good part of the day in shorts and a T-shirt (my treadmill attire) and so when it came time to take a shower, I wanted it to be WARM! I started it out that way and gradually kept turning down the cold so that by the end, it was HOT! The room was full of steam and my skin was red! I never could've gotten into the shower with the water that temperature...I had to get used to it little by little. I was reminded of something that I heard once about a frog and a boiling kettle of water. I can't remember exactly how the story goes, but the gist of it is that if you put a frog in a pot of boiling water, it'll jump right back out. But, if you put the frog in cool water, you'll be able to heat the water to boiling gradually and eventually...I don't know...have frog soup! The point is that the frog doesn't notice the gradual change in temperature until it is ultimately too late!

When our kids were small, and we were in control of their environment, we made sure that it was safe for them...not just physically, but spiritually as well. We were careful about what shows they watched, music they listened to, books they read and words that were said...by them...and by us. We learned early on that words like stupid, dumb and shut-up, even when said in jest, were off limits! As they got older, I remember them wanting to watch movies that other kids were watching...ones that we felt were inappropriate. They tried reasoning with us that these movies didn't contain any language that they hadn't already heard on the bus or at school. We agreed with them, but we also told them that, although we can't always control what we hear and see out in the world, we can control what takes place in our home. We explained to them that we wanted our home to be a safe place...a place where God was honored. We also wanted them to understand that if you continually expose yourself to inappropriate language...whether in movies, music, books or the company you keep...you will gradually get used to it until it is ultimately too late...it will become part of you!

When our kids were younger, we also did work on memorizing Scripture and one of the verses that they all learned was Philippians 4:8..."Whatever is true, whatever is noble, whatever is right, whatever is pure, whatever is lovely, whatever is admirable...if anything is excellent or praiseworthy...think about such things." Such sage advice from our brother Paul! I imagine if he were writing to us today, he would simply say... "Garbage in... Garbage out!"

So, be careful little eyes what you see and little ears what you hear...so you don't end up like our little friend...the frog!

Numbers

I'm a numbers person. You know the type...always counting the days and months it'll be before something special happens. For instance, today is February 25th...2 months from yesterday is Easter, 10 months from today is Christmas and next Wednesday I can say that we're leaving for the beach in 3 months. It's not that I'm wishing the days away...it's just a numbers thing!

I think numbers are interesting. For example, I have an aunt who was born on 11/11 and her daughter on 9/9 and her granddaughter on 7/7 and her sister on 3/3! My grandfather was born in 1899, so his age was always 1 greater than the current year and my grandmother was born in 1901, so her age was always 1 less than the current year. By the way, she died in 7/77 and he died in 8/88. On both sides of my family there were 10 grandchildren...5 boys and 5 girls!

I love playing games with numbers...Sudoku, Kakuro and Ken-Ken...what's not to like? And don't even get me started on the #9...well, maybe just a little about it. The #9 is the most amazing number! When you multiply 9 by the numbers 1-10, the value of the 1st integer in each product increases by 1 and the value of the 2nd integer decreases by one and if you add the integers together in any one product, you get 9. Also, once you go from 5-6 in your multiplying, the integers reverse positions in the products. The #9 is definitely the coolest!

Lately, we've been counting calories...adding them up for each ingredient and then dividing up the total into appropriate-sized portions. We're also in the middle of tax season, which involves a lot of adding and several times a week I get online to balance our checkbook...all things I thoroughly enjoy!

There are some times when numbers disappoint me...like when I go to the gas station or the grocery store and the numbers have gone up again...or when we get our quarterly statement for our pension and the numbers have gone down again. It even bothers me sometimes when I can't count the days until Jesus returns or when I'll meet Him in Heaven. Again, it's not that I'm wishing the days away, it's just that it's hard not to count when you're so used to doing it. That is where faith comes in, trusting God and His timing.

Whether you're a numbers person or not...one thing you can always count on is God. "He is the same yesterday and today and forever." Hebrews 13:8

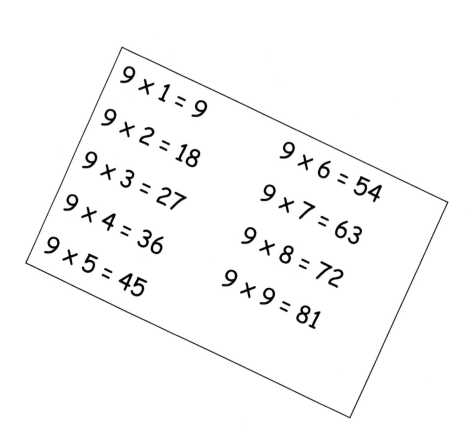

Lighthouse

I love taking trips! I love planning them, mapping them out and searching for different and interesting things to see and do along the way!

I usually prefer to plan trips where we'll be outdoors...checking out waterfalls and amazing gorges...hiking and biking.

I also like to go to historical places...making the trip educational as well as enjoyable...seeing certain man-made structures like the Statue of Liberty, the Brooklyn Bridge and all of the impressive buildings and monuments in our nation's capital.

However, visiting lighthouses meets all the criteria for what I feel makes a great trip...amazing man-made structures with interesting historical stories set in beautiful outdoor venues...and spiritual lessons!

A lighthouse is a fixed point on shore for those who are out in a storm where the wind and waves have turned them around. Hebrews 13:8 says that "Jesus Christ is the same yesterday and today and forever." So, when the storms of life have you turned around, keep your eyes on Him...the only true fixed point in life.

A lighthouse is a light in the darkness, showing us, not only the way to go, but also where not to go. In John 8:12, Jesus said, "I am the light of the world. Whoever follows me will never walk in darkness, but will have the light of life." Let God and His Word light your path and guide your steps.

A lighthouse is a high place where we can get away from everything for a while. God says in Psalm 46:10 to be still so that we can know that He is God. When you are up on top of a lighthouse, it's peaceful and quiet and it's easy to be still...and know that He is God!

In 2010, we climbed the famous lighthouse on the Cape Hatteras National Seashore in North Carolina and in 2011, we climbed one of the twin lighthouses on Thacher Island off the shore of Rockport, Massachusetts.

Thankful at Thanksgiving

Fall has always been one of my favorite seasons. I love the change in the air and the beautiful colors of the leaves. However, it has always been a difficult season for me clothes-wise! I get so used to the easy style of summer...a casual skirt, tank top and a pair of sandals...easy! Or, if we're walking or biking...tennis shoes and a pair of shorts...easy! Fall is tricky for me. I resist giving in to long pants or stockings...until the cold weather really sinks its teeth in, and then I'm fine. I try to hold on to those easy summer styles as long as I can. Unfortunately, someone came up with the idea that it is unacceptable to wear certain colors and clothes after Labor Day, even though the temperatures can remain in the 70's and 80's. (What were they thinking?) This severely limits my choices of clothing for the month of September and even the first few weeks of October and sends me back to my 8th grade days when I stood in front of my closet pondering what to wear while the school bus went by and I had missed it once again! Fortunately, God is gracious and I no longer have to ride a school bus, but there are still places to be and times to be there!

Recently, I sang at a wedding where Chuck was officiating. This meant that Caleb needed to go with us since all of our "sitters" have moved to faraway lands! Chuck needed to be there earlier than I did and so he took off leaving me to get myself ready as well as Caleb. Normally, this shouldn't be a big deal, but this wedding was on a beautiful fall day, and I found myself not only standing in front of *my* closet, but

I'm Thankful

Caleb's as well...pondering! You see, when you add a child into the mix of a new season, you have the added dilemma of finding not only season-appropriate clothes, but also clothes that fit their ever-growing bodies! After several "try-ons", much to Caleb's disgust, we found some clothes that worked and I was off to get in the shower...where I pondered what I would wear, hoping that he would get himself ready. Obviously, at 9, he can dress himself, but cuff buttons and ties can be a problem as well as new shoes that are still a bit stiff. When I got out of the shower, I saw that the clock was getting way too close to "bus time". I hurriedly donned my chosen apparel and began to fix my hair when Caleb walked into my room...all dressed and ready to go. I was so proud! He'd neglected to button the top button under the tie and the shoes needed to be a bit tighter, but he had done his best. I was thankful and we were on time!

  This is usually the part of my article where I introduce a Scripture verse and hopefully parallel my story to a lesson about God, and to tell you the truth, I wasn't sure what the point of all my babbling was this time. But, as I sit here typing, I remember that I'm writing this for the month of November...the month of Thanksgiving...and I am reminded of all the things in my life for which I am truly thankful. I'm thankful that I live in a place where I can experience and appreciate the beauty of each season. I'm thankful for this great country that we live in...for the parts that I've been blessed to see and for the parts that, by the grace of God, I'll get to see. I'm thankful that I still have my Mom and my brother and sister, and that God has moved us around to so many places and has blessed us with so many wonderful friends. I'm thankful for my husband and for my children... thankful for the years that I had with the three older ones and now that they've moved away, thankful that I still have one at home who needs me to help him with his buttons and laces every now and then. Most importantly, I'm thankful for my God who loves me unconditionally...even when I miss the bus!

  1 Thessalonians 5:16-18 says, "Be joyful always; pray continually; give thanks in all circumstances." This is my hope for you this Thanksgiving and always!

Eggs

We celebrate a lot of them. We start off with the New Year and then there's Valentine's Day, St. Patrick's Day, Easter, all of the Patriotic holidays, Halloween, Thanksgiving and finally Christmas. Of those holidays, Easter and Christmas are the ones that are supposed to be all about God, but our society has just turned them into two more money-making, money-spending events. Santa Claus and the Easter Bunny make for tough competition, not to mention the colorful eggs and all that candy!

As Christians, we want our kids to have the fun of decorating eggs and hunting for eggs filled with all kinds of surprises, but we need to make sure that they know the real meaning of Easter. We need to make sure that they understand why we celebrate Easter in the first place. Easter is a time to reflect on how God showed His love for us by making the ultimate sacrifice on our behalf. Is it possible to enjoy the fun of an egg hunt while still remembering God's amazing love and showing it to others?

Recently, I heard about a little 6-year-old girl who went to an Easter egg hunt. She and her 3-year-old brother were happily gathering eggs, when she noticed that another little boy hardly had any eggs in his basket. She told her Mom that she wanted to share some of her eggs with that little boy and she encouraged her little brother to do the same. So, that's what they did. By giving up some of their eggs, they showed love to that little boy and they made a sacrifice on his behalf. "...and a little child shall lead them." ~Isaiah 11:6

By the way...that little girl and her brother are two of our grandchildren, Emily & Daniel. We are so proud of them!

Discover Your Treasure

My story starts way back in 1980. Chuck and I got married on June 7th and we went down to the Outer Banks for a week-long honeymoon. While there we discovered this great mini-golf course at the foot of the sand dunes at Jockey's Ridge...with an impressive castle on one of the holes.

Now fast-forward 30 years: we decided to take our summer vacation down at the Outer Banks to celebrate our 30th Anniversary. We had Caleb with us and we were delighted to re-visit the site of our honeymoon, hoping to show him some of the things we'd enjoyed doing. When we went looking for the mini-golf course, we only found sand. In asking about it, we were told that the sand dunes of Jockey's Ridge had slowly taken over and that the entire course was buried underneath. We decided to take a walk up on the dunes and we found the point of the castle sticking up out of the sand. During the next few years, we went back, only to find that even the high point of the castle was buried.

Now fast-forward eight more years: we got a message from some friends telling us that winter storm Riley blew enough sand away, causing the castle to be exposed...in quite a state of disrepair! But still, it's neat to see it again!

Imagine the number of people who have walked up on those dunes, never realizing what was lying beneath the surface...and imagine their surprise to see this treasure that they never knew existed!

People are like that sand dune. We all have a treasure within us...waiting to be exposed...waiting to be discovered...waiting to be enjoyed. God knows it's there, but the rest of us are surprised when we finally see the treasure that we never knew existed!

What's your treasure? God has put something inside you...inside each of us...and He's waiting for us to discover it and to use it for His glory! Maybe sometimes it takes a storm to blow through our lives and expose it...but when the storm is over...what a treasure is revealed! Discover your treasure!

Turn Your Eyes Upon Jesus

As I settled into the rocking chair with our first newborn, Charlie, I wanted to sing him to sleep. I decided that singing about a cradle falling out of a tree wasn't an option...who makes up songs like that?! I thought about it and settled on the song "Turn Your Eyes Upon Jesus". It has a pleasant, soft tune with a positive message and it immediately became my "go-to" lullaby. I sang it to all four of our children and have sung it to most if not all seven of our grandchildren as well.

As our babies grew, we introduced Bible stories and then moved to memorizing Scripture. We would have family devotions and recite those verses each evening before bed. Our faith was an essential part of who we were and we couldn't help but pass that onto our children. I'll never forget 4-year-old Caitlin reciting "Whatever is true, whatever is noble, whatever is right, whatever is pure, whatever is lovely, whatever is admirable – if anything is excellent or praiseworthy – think about such things." ~ Philippians 4:8, from the arms of her Daddy as they stood at the pulpit in the church where we were serving.

We always encouraged the kids to keep reading their Bibles and we would ask multiple choice Bible trivia questions at the dinner table. They loved it the few times they were able to "stump" their Dad! We would dance around the living room to music by Michael W. Smith and 4-Him. God was like a member of our family!

Now our children are having children of their own and they are passing that faith onto our grandchildren. They are memorizing some of the same verses that our kids did and learning the books of the Bible (Daniel is just finishing up that achievement as I write this article!), and they send us videos of the kids dancing around the living room to Hillsong and Toby Mac. God is still a member of our ever-growing family!

I look at our kids and grandkids and see a family of faithful believers...and I can't help but wonder if part of that is due to singing that lullaby over and over and over to them as I encouraged them to sleep. "Turn your eyes upon Jesus, look full in His wonderful face, and the things of earth will grow strangely dim, in the light of His glory and grace!"

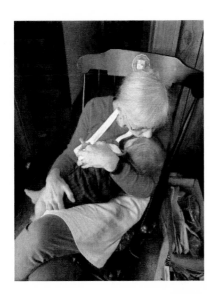

They Are Watching Us!

I remember overhearing Carrie playing one day. She must've been about four and she was doing some serious scolding. When I peeked in to see what was going on, I found that she was scolding her dolls that were supposed to be "sleeping". I reminded her, as always, that when she's pretending, she should pretend about nice things. As I walked away, I realized where she'd learned her behavior: I often had to scold her to get her to stay in bed and to go to sleep. I was ashamed to see my own unbecoming behavior reflected in my daughter.

Just the other day, I was rocking Caleb to sleep for his nap. (We don't rock him at night anymore, but we still do at naptime. He likes it and I know that this special time will soon be gone forever, so...rock on!) He was cuddling his "friend" (a small stuffed lion) and shushing him to sleep with a soft lullaby. Just before he (Caleb) drifted off to sleep, I asked him where he learned to cuddle so well and he said, "From you, Mommy". Now that was music to this mother's ears!

Before you think that I've "evolved" into some super mom over the years, let me tell you that I could easily give you both good and bad examples of my mothering techniques from today as well as 15 years ago. As Solomon would say, "There's nothing new under the sun." However, something I have learned over the years is that people are watching. We, as Christians, are often careful to represent ourselves in a Christ-like way when we're in public, but how about at home? I'm aware that other people are watching my behavior to see if it checks out, but how often do I forget that my children are watching to see if my actions measure up to my words?

Titus 2:7 says this: "In everything set them an example by doing what is good. In your teaching show integrity, seriousness and soundness of speech that cannot be condemned, so that those who oppose you may be ashamed because they have nothing bad to say about us." In other words, we're to do our best (with God's help) to live our lives above reproach and in a Christ-like way, so that those who are watching us may have a good example to follow.

During this time of Lent and Easter and in the months to come, may we set ourselves apart for God and may our lives be a reflection of God's love to all that are watching!

Heroes

Did you have any heroes when you were growing up? Some kids have fictional heroes, like Batman or Superman. Charlie probably won't like the fact that I'm telling you this, but he had these red shorts and a blue shirt and a cape that I made him and he would "fly" around the house saving the day!

Some kids have historical heroes, like Abraham Lincoln or Neil Armstrong (I'm glad Charlie didn't try to be like him!) Some kids even have Biblical heroes, like David or Peter...trying to walk across their wading pools!

Whether you know it or not, all kids have heroes...their parents! Even though they fight us at times and try to resist our authority, a lot of what they say and do, they get from us! Unfortunately, they not only learn the good things but the bad things as well. Some kids look at their Mom and Dad and see a loving couple and learn how to treat others. Sadly though, some kids see a Dad who's always hitting their Mom and they figure that this is the way things are supposed to be.

We need to realize, as parents, the enormous influence that we have on our children and accept that responsibility. Once we've done this, we may need to make some changes in our lives. Ask Chuck about the time that he climbed up into his Dad's lap while he was smoking a pipe and asked, "Daddy, when will I be big enough to smoke a pipe like you?" Chuck's Dad made a decision to quit smoking then and there. He realized his influence and he realized his responsibility and he acted accordingly.

Sometimes, the change we need to make will involve getting rid of something in our lives...like a bad habit or vulgar language or a bad attitude. Sometimes, though, this change may involve adding something to our lives. Proverbs 22:6 says, "Train up a child in the way he should go, and when he is old, he will not depart from it." Now, we can *tell* our kids all the things necessary for them to live their lives right, but unless we become living examples of the right way to live, chances are that most of our words won't stick! It's great to encourage your children to pray, but the best way for them to learn is for you to show them. Let them hear you pray. It's great for you to want to bring your children to Sunday school when they're little, but not if you merely drop them off and go back home. As they get older and start to think more for themselves, they will see that Sunday school isn't a priority in your life...so why should it be in theirs?

I could go on and on about the positive and negative influences we have on our children! Please think about these things, as I have been, and let's evaluate the examples that we're setting for our kids...as long as we're heroes in their eyes anyway, let's try to be superheroes!

Hanging a Cling

It all started when I was decorating the house for Easter. I went to hang a "cling" in the window and I decided that I'd better clean the window first. So, I got out a rag and the glass cleaner and a few minutes later, I had a clean window...on the inside anyway. You can't appreciate the cleanness of a window if only one side is clean...so, outside I went. In order to clean the window, I had to remove the screen, which I noticed was also dirty. Once I had the window clean, the shutters looked like they needed a good scrubbing, as did the rest of the woodwork on the porch. The table and chairs which had been stored there over the winter were filthy and while I was at it, I hosed down the floor of the porch too. By the time I was done, my whole front porch was clean. All I had intended to do was to hang an Easter cling in the window. Amazing how one thing can lead to another.

You know, giving your life to Christ is a lot like my porch-cleaning excursion. God doesn't expect our whole "porch" to be clean right away. He starts with one area, one window, one thing in our lives that needs a good cleaning and then He encourages us to allow one thing to lead to another. Before we know it, He's changed our whole life and like a clean porch, it's for the better.

In Psalm 51:10, King David says, "Create in me a clean heart, O God, and renew a right spirit within me." There were times in David's life when he couldn't see the sin in his life, but once God began to show it to him, it all became clear and he wanted his heart to be pure.

Oh, I forgot to mention that I didn't realize how dirty my window was...or my whole porch for that matter...until I took that first step to clean it up. Choose one area of your life and allow God to "clean it up". You'll be amazed at how one thing can lead to another!

The Blankie

Isn't it wonderful when someone takes the time to tell you something nice about your children? When Charlie, Carrie and Caitlin were little, we didn't go out to eat very often. However, several times when we did eat out, a couple (usually elderly) would stop by to tell us how well-behaved our children were! We were so proud! (Of course, there were other times when we couldn't get out of there fast enough!)

The other day, someone, a member of our church, had something nice to share about Caleb. She told me that she was standing outside after church when Caleb opened the door and asked her what she was doing. She said that she was waiting for her daughter and that if he saw her to tell her to hurry because she was cold. He shut the door and stood there for about 30 seconds...thinking. Then, he opened the door and offered her his "blankie", also letting her know that she couldn't go anywhere with it. She wrapped it around her neck and was not only warmed by the blanket, but by the gesture as well.

As mothers, we can spend many of our days waiting for them to be over...picking up toys, breaking up quarrels, listening to whining, shuttling our kids back and forth...well, you get the picture. Many days, we want to escape to a nice, warm, quiet place, but it's moments like the "blankie" incident that make it all worthwhile.

As you celebrate this Mother's Day, may we remember the good things and know that we are blessed!

P.S. For those of you who know Caleb and his attachment to his "blankie", you also know that this lady was warmed by the fiercely-protective stare of a little boy who did the right thing, albeit, reluctantly!

They Imitate Us!

So, we're standing in the check-out line at Wal-Mart. There's a man in front of us and as his items move forward, we begin to unload our cart. Pre-occupied with this process, we initially fail to notice what Caleb is "up to". As we put our remaining items up on the belt, we realize that the man in front of us has a cat. We realize this because he is purchasing numerous (24 according to Caleb) cans of cat food. We especially notice this because Caleb is busying himself by stacking the cans into neat piles. I make a comment that he is my son...to which Chuck readily agrees...and since that's the case, I mention to Caleb that he should have been stacking them according to color and kind. HORRIFIED, he begins re-stacking them that way...to which Chuck comments, "Oh my gosh, he really is just like you!"

We have four children and they are all different...all possessing a different combination of qualities...some mine, some Chuck's and some all their own! It's fun to watch them as they grow...to see certain characteristics emerge and to recognize them as ones they've inherited from you. Kids inherit all kinds of things from eye color to personality traits. Maybe they have our smile or run the same way we do. Yes, many things are inherited, but some things are taught or "caught". Children often imitate what they see. For example, children of good readers often become good readers. Unfortunately, this can work in a negative way as well. Parents who lose their temper or swear will many times produce children who do the same. We, as parents, have a huge responsibility to develop good qualities in ourselves so that our children will "catch" them from us.

Faith is one of those things that is not inherited...it is learned by example. Children who are brought up in a home where the Scriptures are read and where prayers are said are much more likely to be people of faith as they grow and mature. I think it's funny when Caleb stacks cat food cans by color or when Charlie alphabetizes his DVDs (that's another story!), but it's humbling when Caleb breaks into a song of praise in the middle of a prayer or when Charlie witnesses to a co-worker. I'm glad that I passed on my love for math, but I'm eternally grateful that I passed on my love for the Lord.

Read Proverbs 31 and have a Happy Mother's Day!

Motherhood

I don't know about you, but waiting for Caleb to pick up his room so that I can clean it is like waiting for the return of Christ...you're not sure if it's ever going to happen in your lifetime! So, the other day I decided that I'd waited long enough and began the task of putting his things where they belong so that I could dust and sweep the room. I noticed that the things left out were different than the ones that used to be...his taste in playthings had matured. I especially noticed how dusty the cowboy hat and boots were. It used to be that they were worn every day and I wondered when that had changed. Funny how some changes cause us to celebrate while others cause us to be very reflective and possibly even sad. For instance, "let the celebration begin!" when they sleep through the night, when you change the last diaper, when they can feed themselves and when they finally figure out how to chase that rabbit around the tree and their shoes stay tied! However, it's a whole different story when you pack away that favorite sleeper, when they don't even remember who Steve from "Blues Clues" is, when they're no longer interested in "Candy Land" or "Good Night Moon", and the favorite stuffed animal (the one you had to buy three of because it kept getting lost!) is at the bottom of the toy box!

> Motherhood is such a
> roller coaster ride

Motherhood is such a roller coaster ride! When you start out, you hear the word "Mommy" so often, you wish you could change your name and you keep all of your favorite magazines in the bathroom because it's the only place you might be able to be alone. As they get older, you're so busy being doctor, teacher, disciplinarian, and chauffer, you forget how to be wife and lover. Then, before you know it, they're heading off to college, walking down the aisle and having children of their own and you remember rocking them to sleep and kissing their "boo-boos" like it was yesterday!

Now, before we all start to cry, God reminds us in Ecclesiastes that everything has a time and season. I love having the memories of when the kids were small, but it's also exciting to see them take off on their own...knowing you did an "OK" job of raising them. It's neat when Caleb is reciting Scripture verses that he's memorizing and Carrie walks in and joins him because she remembers learning that verse when she was his age. And just when you feel like you're not needed anymore, the kids get past that "know it all" stage and come to you for advice on things like majors and jobs and wedding dresses, not to mention when they fail a class or lose a job...or a love.

Yes, being a mother is a full-time, highly varied, and emotionally draining task...and one of the most rewarding experiences a woman can have...and I wouldn't trade a moment of it! By the way, after I lamented about the dusty cowboy hat and how much Caleb has grown up, I looked under the bed and found 8 paper towel tubes, 6 pencils, 2 shoes and a pair of underwear. Then, he came home from school with his lunch box in his backpack...dripping from the open drink box that he'd brought home...and I counted to 10...and then counted my blessings!

My Privilege

I'm not running for President of the United States. I'm not the CEO of a big corporation. I'll never make it to the final round of American Idol. I'm a Mom...and a stay-at-home Mom, at that!

As I look back on my life, I don't regret the choices I've made...even though I did have some questions along the way. You see, my adult years have taken place during a time when most women have careers or jobs...whether it be by choice or necessity. Our society tends to measure a person's success by things like: occupational accomplishments, power and superiority, not to mention annual gross income. Consequently, there have been times when I focused on society's values and felt that I had come up short...that my life was a waste...that I was a failure.

When Caitlin (my youngest at the time) entered 1st grade, the question on everyone's mind was, "What are you going to do with your time now that the kids are all in school?" I wrestled with the answer to that question and even went to work part-time when she was in 3rd grade. It started out as an "ideal" week-day only job, but by the end there were nights and weekends involved as well as a few holidays...not so "ideal".

When Caleb came along, that problem was solved for a while and now he's in 3rd grade and I can't say that I haven't pondered the possibility of getting a job...but, he needs me on those unexpected snow days when there's snowmen to be created and hot chocolate to be enjoyed. He needs me for 3 months of summer days so we can go for walks and ride our bikes...so we can play one more game of "Sorry" or even sit on the porch swing and enjoy reading the latest tales of Peter Pan or Captain Jack Sparrow. He needs me to be there when he has to stay home from school because he's sick and he loves the fact that every year I get to chaperone his school field trip!

I've gone from tucking them in at night, to teaching them to tie their shoes, to helping them prepare their taxes. I've watched them go from riding off on a two-wheeler to driving off in a car (well, 3 of them, at least). Whether I'm sending them off to the neighborhood school or off to college in West Virginia or off to live in Texas or Oklahoma...I'm still the one they call "Mom" and I'm still here for them. I'm only a phone call away and I have the privilege of being one of the biggest prayer warriors they have!

No, I haven't come up short and I haven't wasted my life. On the contrary, I've been blessed beyond measure...I'm a Mom...no, I'm the best Mom on earth...it says so right there in crayon on my refrigerator door! And if you're a Mom...blessings and congratulations!

Plan B

Last Thursday, we had our Parsonage Dinner for April. I had the menu all planned out ahead of time, got my shopping done and was ready to go, when the power went out. I had things that I could do which didn't require electricity, but as the morning turned to afternoon; I realized that I needed to come up with a "Plan B" for the menu...which included an alternate means of preparation. Chuck came home from work and got the fire ring going and began to prepare the grill and just as I got into my new groove...the power came back on. So, it was back to "Plan A" and we had a wonderful evening!

The next day was Chuck's birthday and we had been talking about going to the Japanese Steak House in Johnstown...until Caitlin mentioned that she wanted to meet us for dinner in Greensburg (our halfway point between Pittsburgh and Jennerstown), which is not near Johnstown at all. So, he decided on Red Lobster in Greensburg...until we discovered that Caitlin was too tired from her previous day's whirlwind trip to Philadelphia and back. We told her to stay put and decided to go with our original plan. When we got to the mall where the Japanese Steak House is located, we discovered that the power was out in the whole mall and most of the surrounding out-parcels...except for Red Lobster! So, we went back to "Plan A", which didn't work and then went back to "Plan B", except for it being a different Red Lobster...which I guess makes it a "Plan C"! At any rate, we had a wonderful evening!

I'm sorry if this is a bit confusing, but life isn't always neat and tidy. In fact, it can get rather messy at times, throwing us curves that we're not always sure how to handle. Life's unpredictability isn't always about trivial things like how to fix dinner or where to eat it. Sometimes those curves can be about things that are of the utmost importance...things like bankruptcy or illness, or your company downsizing or even death. Oh, we can make an attempt at preparing for our unknown future by buying insurance and contributing to an IRA, but the best way to prepare is by spending time with the One to whom the future is not an unknown...God!

John 3:16 says that God loves everyone in the whole world, Jeremiah 29:11 says that God has plans for each one of us and Matthew 28:20 says that Jesus will be with us always. Now, if He loves us, then His plans for us must be good, so we need to trust in that love and trust in those plans...trust in His Word, so that when those curves come, we can face them head on and finish well just like Paul said in 2 Timothy 4:7.

One other thing to remember: sometimes God calms the storm like He did in Luke 8, but sometimes He stands in the fire with us like He did in Daniel 3. Either way, He promises to be with us...and God never needs a "Plan B"!

In His Presence

Chuck and I both got a text from our daughter, Carrie, the other day: our "almost 4-year-old" granddaughter, Emily, "missed us terribly" and wanted to know if we could get on Skype (a program on the computer that enables you to see who you're talking to). I think it had been a week since we had done this because of busy schedules, so we told her to give us a call later and that we would love to see and talk to them!

Later that evening, we got on Skype and Emily was "front and center" to say hello...for about 30 seconds...then she was off to play...but still within "earshot" of the computer. We coaxed her over a couple of times to talk to her, but basically, I think she was just happy to "be in our presence", so to speak.

When we did talk to her, she was reassured of our love for her and we also talked to her about some things to come: we'll be heading to the beach in June and it will be Emily's first time. It's fun to tell her how wonderful it will be...digging for sand crabs, searching for sea shells, running in and out of the waves, playing mini-golf and even climbing the Cape Hatteras Lighthouse...but because Emily has never been to the beach, she has to trust us as to just how wonderful it will be...she has to take our word for it until she is able to experience it for herself! Skype is wonderful and we are so thankful that we are able to see them in this way...but we always look forward to the times when we can see each other "face to face"!

Isn't that just like our relationship with God? Life gets busy and sometimes days go by when we don't talk to Him. We find ourselves "missing Him terribly" and we have a strong desire to "be in His presence".

When we do come before God, He assures us of His love for us and He delights in telling us about the things to come: "In my Father's house are many rooms; if it were not so, I would have told you. I am going there to prepare a place for you." ~Jesus, as written in John 14:2. "Then I saw a new heaven and a new earth...the Holy City...prepared as a bride beautifully dressed for her husband...God Himself will be with His people...He will wipe every tear from their eyes...there will be no more death or mourning or crying or pain..." ~excerpts from Revelation 21

We, like Emily, have to trust God as to how wonderful life with Him will be...we have to take Him at His Word until we are able to experience it for ourselves...and then we shall see Him face to face!

What Love Is All About

As you know, June is the month when we celebrate Father's Day. In our house, that's a pretty special day; one in which the kids specifically honor their Dad by saying, "I love you" and by thanking God for him in their prayers and by giving him the kind of cards that you can't find in any Hallmark store: the home-made kind!

Well, June is special to us for another reason: it's the month when we celebrate our anniversary. This year (1996) will be our 16th! Let me share with you a few things about the man I married and the father of my children.

First and foremost, Chuck is a man after God's own heart. He loves the kids and me very much but he loves the Lord most...and that's as it should be. I wouldn't have it any other way because by loving God first, Chuck is able to love us far better than he could on his own. He's free to love us with the love of God. Let me illustrate.

Last February, Chuck went to a Promise Keepers gathering for pastors down in Atlanta over Valentine's Day. Now, those of you who know me know that I like to make a big deal out of those small days and I was sad to know that my valentine wouldn't be here with me. When that special day arrived, so did a dozen red roses: a very extravagant gift! As much as I loved and appreciated those roses, what touched me even more were the notes that I received each day in the mail. He'd written them ahead of time and had someone mail them to me each day. That's thoughtfulness.

Most of you also know that I do most of the cooking for the family (and for the most part, we're better off that way!) but, on occasion, Chuck has been known to make dinner in order to surprise me or just to give me a break. Even though I could probably make it better myself, I recognize this as a true expression of his love for me because it isn't one of his strengths and he doesn't even pretend to like doing it! That's sacrifice.

Both of these examples of what love is all about: putting someone else's interest before your own. Both of these are examples of how Jesus loves us and wants us to love others. Although these gestures were aimed particularly at me, they spilled over onto the kids as well. By Chuck's example, Charlie is learning how to show love to a wife and Carrie and Caitlin are seeing qualities that they should be looking for in a husband. Granted, they won't need this knowledge for quite a few years, but you can't wait until they're ready to walk down the aisle to show them what to look for in a mate. Proverbs 22:6 says to "Train up a child in the way he should go and when he is old, he will not depart from it." Chuck and I feel that this training begins even before the child is born. Praying for your children and setting good, Christ-like examples start long before they can understand your words.

We also read in the Bible where Jesus said to "Let the little children come..." and Chuck has always tried to make time in his busy schedule to spend time with the kids: from "this little piggy" to piggy-back rides; from "wrestle-mania" in the living room to airplane rides into bed; from games of Candy Land to games of run-down in the back yard.

The kids and I have been blessed with a godly man who shows us Christ by the way that he lives his life. Happy Anniversary, Honey! Happy Father's Day, Dad! We love you!

What's Inside?

One of our former parsonages had a large living room and dining room...all paneled. The windows were narrow and the drapes were heavy. All of that combined made for a bit of a dreary area. We've gone back to visit several times in the 22 years since we left and they have done some extensive remodeling. The paneling has been removed...uncovering a fireplace with a mantle in the living room and a built-in China cabinet in the dining room! We had no idea that those treasures were hiding under there...although I'm quite sure that someone did.

When our current parsonage was remodeled a couple of years ago, an addition was made by opening up the dining room. Part of the outside brick wall was now inside. The plan was to cover up the brick with drywall and plaster to match the rest of the new walls...until I approached the contractor and convinced him that an exposed brick wall would lend a "homey" touch to the place. I'm so glad that this treasure was not hidden and that it is here to be enjoyed and appreciated.

For those who are Christians, we have a treasure inside of us. Paul says in 2 Corinthians 4 that "God made His light shine in our hearts...and we have this treasure (Jesus) in jars of clay (us)" and Jesus said in Matthew 5 that we need to "let our light shine before men" that God may be praised and glorified!

Don't hide your treasure! You may not realize that it's there...but God does and He wants you to let it shine so that others may come to know Him and have His light within them too!

Summer

That word carries a lot of different connotations for different people. For students (and teachers), summer means a break from the school routine. For pastors, it means a lighter meeting load and smaller congregations on Sundays. For farmers, summer is a time of planting, cultivating and preparing for the harvest. For me, summer means all those things and more. Summer is definitely a break from the school routine...a break from getting up so early and helping with all kinds of homework. Summer means a lighter activity load for the kids, which means less "chauffeuring" for me. Summer is the largest block of time I have with my children for planting and cultivating those seeds of faith...preparing them for the harvest of a rich future and a life-long relationship with the Lord. Summer is a time for strengthening family ties and for building memories to last a lifetime.

Summer is a time for strengthening family ties and for building memories

---

I saw an ad the other day of a little girl wearing a graduation cap and gown that were way too big for her. The caption under the picture said, "In about five minutes your child will be on their way to college." Now that's fast! Come the middle of May, Charlie will be returning home from college...his first year behind him. Come the first part of June, Carrie will be heading into her senior year of High School and Caitlin, her freshman year. Of course, Caleb is still at home with me, but in about five minutes, we'll be sending him off too! The time we have with our children goes so fast. You couldn't have convinced me of that 14 years ago when I had three preschoolers, but you know what they say about hindsight...

Spend the summer together. Plan lots of things to do together, whether you go out of town or stay in your own backyard. Have some family devotions, and, speaking as a pastor's wife, take a vacation from the world and all its pressures, not from spending time in God's House and His Word. Here is some Scripture to get you started on those devotions:

Deuteronomy 4:9, 6:5-9, 11:18-21

Joshua 24:15   Matthew 19:14

Mark 10:14, Luke 18:16

John 3:16-21   Acts 12:1-19

Jesus' "I Am" statements: John 6:35, 8:12, 10:7-10, 10:11-18, 11:25-26, 14:6-7

Ephesians 4,5 & 6

Philippians 2:12-16, 3:12-14, 4:4-8

Colossians 3:1-25:

The whole book of James (for serious study!)

Summer. Make it one of growth and fun. Make it one to remember!

Waiting

Have you ever thought about how much of our lives are spent waiting? We wait in line at the grocery store. We wait in traffic for the light to change. We wait for our turn to see the doctor in, of all places, the waiting room! We recently waited for the leaves to change color and now we're waiting for them to fall off the trees so they can be raked up. We wait for the first snowflakes of winter, with mixed emotions, and for the first crocuses of spring. We're waiting for Thanksgiving and Christmas and in a year, the start of a new millennium. Our family is anxiously awaiting the arrival of a new family member. We wait for all kinds of things each and every day and sometimes, most times, the waiting is difficult! We can easily become irritated and impatient!

The Bible has something to say about waiting. Isaiah 40:31 says, "Those who wait upon the Lord shall renew their strength. They will soar on wings like eagles; they will run and not grow weary; they will walk and not be faint."

Our world encourages instant gratification and we, therefore, often times expect everything to happen quickly. We want instant answers to our questions and our wishes met immediately. God, however, does things in His own timing. He stresses the importance of patience and tells us to WAIT on Him. With God, waiting is a good thing if done in an appropriately patient way.

So, next time you're waiting in traffic or the line at the grocery store, think about how God would want you to wait!

The Rescued Relationship

It seems like yesterday...but it happened 11 years ago. It was 1993. Charlie and Carrie were in school all day and Caitlin was attending morning Kindergarten. Chuck was at work and I had a little bit of freedom for the first time in over 10 years! Caitlin left on the bus with the other kids and a bus brought her home as well (not so in most places). The bus dropped her off right in front of our house and she would always come in the front door. (I'm telling you this for future reference.)

So, I had about three hours to myself. I could do housework. I could sew. I could go shopping...all by myself. That was an amazing concept to me at the time. I hadn't done anything alone on a regular basis for a very long time. One day, 11 years ago, I decided to go to the nearby Giant Eagle for some groceries. I arrived at the store and got a cart. I didn't have to look around for a child-sized cart because I didn't have any children with me. You see, this particular store had small carts that were exact replicas of the adult-sized ones and Caitlin always liked pushing her cart alongside of mine. I remember feeling a little strange that day...no children...I wasn't sure how I felt about that. But, I "trudged on" and tried to make the best of it. After all, I'd been looking forward to this day for a long time. I thought about how quickly I could get my shopping done without someone trailing along next to me, but instead, I found myself moving at a very leisurely pace. Maybe it was because I was savoring the moment or maybe it was because it was the pace I was used to. Either way, I took my good old sweet time...a little too much time and found myself leaving a little later than I wanted. I made my purchases and headed home.

On a good traffic day, I could easily make it home in 10 minutes. Of course, this wasn't that day. I had someone in front of me who wasn't even going the speed limit and there were no passing zones. I grew more and more frantic as the minutes passed by and as I came to the conclusion that I wasn't going to make it back on time. There were no cell phones and even if I'd had one, there was no one to call. Our neighbors worked and Chuck was at the office, four miles away (I was closer than that!). Finally, I pulled up in front of the house and I saw a little girl coming down the steps to the side door. This meant that she'd already tried the front door, as usual, and upon finding it locked, decided to try the side door...only to find it locked as well. As I pulled up and our eyes met, we both burst into tears. I felt like the worst mother in the whole world. I vowed that I would never let that happen again and it never did...until...

Eleven years later, I have another Kindergartener. Caleb gets driven to school by 8:30am and is picked up at 11:15am. (I'm telling you this for future reference.) Last week after dropping him off at school and taking Carrie to her 9:30 class at Community College, I decided to stop in at Wal-Mart before having to pick Caleb up. I checked my watch and it was 10:00am, giving me about ½ hour to shop. The next time I looked at my watch, it was 11:00am! I don't know where the time went, but I knew that I didn't have enough time to check out and get to Caleb on time. I raced to Customer service, explaining my situation and leaving the cart with them, I ran to the car. I, once again, drove as fast as traffic allowed. I grew more and more frantic as the minutes passed by and as I came to the conclusion that I wasn't going to make it on time. "Lord, I vowed that I would never do this again and I've let everyone down. Please forgive my transgression and do something to help me. I'm desperate, Lord. Amen."

> Lord, please forgive my transgressions and do something to help me.

Let me give you a little more information for future reference. I usually get to school to pick Caleb up between 11:00am and 11:05am. The bus arrives every day between 11:05am and 11:10am and the kids come walking out the door at 11:15am.

As I turned into the driveway of the school, my watch read 11:17am! I pulled up to the school...no bus. I figured that the bus had already gone and that I had a crying child inside. Then, I saw another Mom waiting outside and she said that the kids had not been dismissed yet. As we spoke, the bus pulled up and the kids were dismissed. Somehow, someway, my prayers had been answered. It's as if God had stopped time again like He did when Joshua needed more time to defeat the Amorites and the sun stood still. (See Joshua 10). For whatever reason, God had seen fit to spare me, to spare Caleb.

This doesn't sound much like a Thanksgiving article, but I am truly thankful for an answered prayer and a rescued relationship.

We Have The Same Shoes!

So, I was walking Caleb home from school one day and he was trying to tell me something about one of his classmates. He wanted to relay a funny story and he told me that the boy's name was James. I was trying to get a handle on who this boy was, but the school year had just started and I wasn't yet familiar with all of the other 1st graders. Caleb could see that I was having trouble and he said, "You know Mom, the boy who has the same shoes as I have." Needless to say, that didn't help! Just then, Caleb's name was being called from behind us and as we turned to see who it was, Caleb said, "It's James! Now you can see who I mean." Now, given the demographics of our small town...the 1st thing I noticed about James was not his shoes...James was Black (or African American). As the boy came closer, the 2nd thing I noticed about him was a birthmark on one of his eyebrows...making that eyebrow twice the size of the other one.

Caleb had overlooked two very distinguishing characteristics of his new-found friend. To Caleb, James was just another boy...who happened to have the same shoes! As we celebrate Thanksgiving this month, let's think back to that 1st Thanksgiving where the Pilgrims ate with the Indians (or Native Americans). They overlooked each other's differences and focused on what they had in common. They shared their gifts and talents and blessings.

Galatians 3:28 says that no matter what our background or station in life...we are all one in Christ. In Matthew 18:3, Jesus says that we all must change and become like children in order to enter the kingdom of heaven.

Let's take our cue from a 1st grader and know that we are all children of God..."Red and yellow black and white, we are precious in His sight."

Purses

Over the years, I've carried many different purses...but they have shared a common purpose: to allow me to take along anything that I might deem necessary to be prepared for any situation that might arise!

I got my first purse in the mid-'60's. It was white with a little daisy on it and I used it to carry a hankie and my gloves to church.

In the mid-'70's, my purse was made out of suede and had fringe on it. I used it to carry a hair brush and make-up to High School.

In the mid-'80's, my purse became a diaper bag and I had various designs over the years. I used them to carry diapers, wipes, bottles, pacifiers, toys, books, cheerios and a change of clothes or two...along with my personal items and all of the other "stuff" that the other members of the family didn't want to carry!!

In the mid-'90's, I was back to a purse and I opted for a teeny tiny one that was barely big enough for my wallet and sunglasses...because I was tired of carrying everyone else's "stuff"!

"A woman who fears the Lord is to be praised".

"A woman who fears the Lord is to be praised." ~Proverbs 31:30

These days, I have an assortment of purses...different sizes and colors to fit the occasion...my favorite being a gift from my husband that is big enough to carry the following: wallet and sunglasses, chap stick and hairbrush, nail clippers and band-aids, hand lotion and hand sanitizer, pocket calendar and phone, shopping lists and coupons, safety pin and sewing kit, breath mints and ibuprofen...well, you get the idea! My goodness, I can even throw in my Kindle, a bottle of water and my latest crocheting project!!

The point of this pondering is that women like to be prepared for anything that might come up...and I know a certain husband who's been glad, more than a few times, that I carry all the things that I do! However, as good as it is to be prepared for all of *life's little emergencies*, nothing compares to being prepared for *life itself*...and that doesn't involve packing a purse, it involves spending time daily in God's Word and in prayer! When we walk with the Lord...growing in wisdom and faith...we *really* have what we need to be prepared for any situation that might arise!

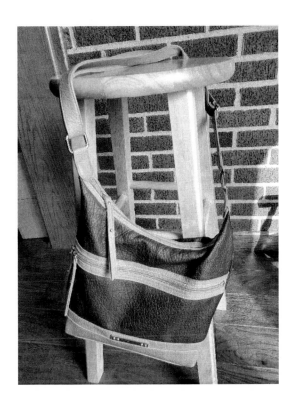

The Best Choice

It finally happened. I dropped my smart phone and cracked the top left quarter of my screen. The phone still worked, but it was difficult to slide my finger across the screen and I was concerned about putting it up to my ear, for fear of getting fragments of the screen in my hair. I was well aware of the availability of cases and screen protectors. I just didn't like the bulk of the cases and just hadn't bothered with the other. This was my second smart phone and I figured I'd been getting along just fine as I was. I also chose not to pay the monthly fee for insurance...I now see that I made some poor choices!

He is able to use my life to further his Kingdom

Fortunately, our phone company was able to cover my damaged screen with a hard, clear screen protector and I am able to use my phone...I just have to look past the cracks! I'm just thankful that my phone wasn't damaged beyond repair. Sometimes it takes something bad happening to help us recognize our poor choices and to do something about it!

I know I've not always made the best choices in life and many times, I've suffered the consequences of my poor choices, but thankfully, I made a choice a long time ago to let Jesus be my Lord and Savior and He is able to use my life to further His Kingdom...even if people have to look through the cracks and scars to see Him!

How about you? Maybe you're aware of who Jesus is, but you've just not bothered to make Him part of your life. Maybe you feel that you won't like the changes that will take place in your life if you invite Him in. Maybe you figure that you've been getting along just fine as you are...

Maybe, you've already chosen to live for Jesus, and that is awesome, but maybe you haven't. Someday, something is going to come along to make you realize that by ignoring Jesus, you've made a poor choice. Hopefully it will be some partial damage that encourages you to allow Jesus to cover your sins with His protection. But it may be something more...something that damages you beyond repair.

Don't make the same mistake I made with my phone...after all, it's just a phone.

The Power Outage

I had a very unexpected and "strange" day this week. Penelec needed to work on a transformer in the area and had scheduled a total power outage from 9am-Noon. It actually lasted until 12:30pm.

I didn't hear about this until the day before and at first, I wondered if it was a joke. I had never heard of nor experienced anything like this in my life! At any rate, I decided to take the day off since 95% of my work involves using the computer and making copies, neither of which I would be able to do.

I got up in the morning and got ready for the day, giving thanks for the sunshine since I wouldn't be able to turn on any lights.

I had decided that I would clean out some of my kitchen cupboards and pantry, re-organizing and tossing away things that had overstayed their welcome, noted by their long-past expiration dates!

At 9:03am, the power went out. I was amazed at how quiet it was in the house! No refrigerator running, no furnace running, no computer running.

As I adjusted to this new kind of quiet, I began to hear our clocks ticking. We actually have quite a few battery-operated clocks in the house because I always wanted to make sure that our kids could tell time that way and not just the digital way. I'd forgotten how pretty they sounded.

Those clocks are there all the time, but their comforting presence is drowned out by the constant noises of life.

God is with us all the time too, but we often let life drown out His comforting presence as well. Life has many things to distract us from hearing God.

Take time to find a quiet place each day so that you can hear God's voice as He speaks to you, letting you know that He is always with you, giving you His comfort and peace!

Unplugged

Chuck and I recently took advantage of a beautiful Sunday afternoon and went for a bike ride on the nearby Ghost Town Trail. We rode from Blacklick to Heshbon, which took us along the Blacklick Creek. Because of the abundance of rain we've had, the creek was running high and swiftly, creating the most beautiful sound...as beautiful as the waves crashing up on the shore of the ocean.

One of the things we like about the bike trail is saying "hello" to those we pass and, occasionally, striking up a nice conversation. That day, we did just that. However, at one point we passed three people in a row with earbuds on. Evidently, they were listening to music and, therefore, could not hear us when we said "hello". It occurred to me that they also couldn't hear the beautiful sound coming from the creek. They were "plugged in" instead of being "tuned in".

The writer of Psalm 66:4 says, "All the earth bows down to You; they sing praise to You, they sing praise to Your name."

Paul says in Romans 1:20, "For since the creation of the world God's invisible qualities-His eternal power and divine nature-have been clearly seen, being understood from what has been made, so that men are without excuse."

According to these verses, we can find God in the things that He has created. When we are enjoying nature, we need to be "unplugged" from the world and "tuned in" to the message that God has for us through His marvelous creation!

Content and the Coin-Operated Car

Caleb and I were shopping at Wal-Mart the other day (not a surprise!) and, as usual, he asked if he could ride the coin-operated car (not a surprise!). As usual, I told him that if he was a good boy in the store, he could have a ride before we leave (again, not a surprise!).

As we walked through the store, all he could talk about was taking that ride! When we were done checking out, I told him that he could have a ride because he'd been a good boy. We walked over to the car; I put down my bags and reached in my purse for my wallet. The car takes $.50 (two quarters) to make it run. I had one quarter and multiple dimes, nickels and pennies. Not only did I not want to disappoint Caleb, I did not want him to make a scene in the store. I said a quick prayer and gently told him that I didn't have the right kind of money to make the car work and I waited for his response. He said, "That's okay, Mommy. I'll just pretend that the car is on." (Now that was a surprise!)

I was so amazed and impressed by the maturity of his response! He was content to merely sit on the car, making all the appropriate noises and smiling as if the car was on.

I was reminded of the verse where Paul says that he has learned to be content whatever the circumstances. (Philippians 4:12) Life doesn't always go as planned. It's full of disappointments and changes, but, as Christians, we need to learn to weather through the disappointments and changes all the while standing firm on Christ, our foundation. When things don't go our way, we need to make the best of it and remember that our responses to our circumstances need to be a reflection of Christ, not of our sinful nature.

Sometimes, God brings about those changes, and if that's the case, they're for our good! (Now that's _not_ a surprise!)

I Forgot to Study!

So, how do you deal with your child when they come down to the breakfast table and announce that they'd forgotten to study for the test they have that day? Many reactions come to mind: anger, frustration, helplessness. What do you do? You can try to help them study and encourage them to use what little time they have wisely. You can assure them that you'll be praying for them and suggest they do the same. (Of course, this is just a hypothetical situation. Our children are always prepared and on time! If you believe that, I'd like to talk to you about this little bridge that I have for sale...)

This is indeed a very frustrating situation and while it doesn't happen all the time, it happens too often for my taste (and sanity!). Getting back to the thought of praying for them, the question arises: "Should we pray for our children when this happens?" Do they deserve to enter a plea to God when they haven't given it their best shot? When a child diligently studies for a test, it only seems right that we should go to God on their behalf, praying that they'll be able to think clearly and remember the things that they've gone over so many times.

But what about when they haven't been so diligent? Is it right for us to ask God to intervene by miraculously filling their heads with knowledge? I've struggled with that problem over the years and have come to the conclusion that the answer is "Yes." No one deserves to receive anything from God and it is when we "mess up" or sin that we need Him most. Now, I'm not suggesting that we ask God to give them an "A" when no effort has been shown, but that He help them to relax and recall the things they've read and discussed in class and that they maybe learn a lesson from this. This, my friends, is called grace. The definition of grace is "unmerited favor". No one deserves God's grace, but He gives it because He loves us.

By the way, a certain child of ours received a heaping portion of God's grace because this test was an open book test! God is so gracious to the undeserving!

The Gar-Be-Gar

O ur son, Caleb, will be 21 months old on the 8th of October. My, how time flies! Spending most of my day in "Caleb's world" is a time full of laughter and surprises. He's becoming quite the little chatterbox and attempts to say just about everything. Of course, like any toddler, he has his own language and I, like any foreign exchange student, am, out of necessity, picking up words here and there to enhance our daily conversations.

Let me share a few of his favorite words with you in case you find yourself conversing with Caleb. I'll try to spell these phonetically to aid in your pronunciation.

"Ah-chee" means juice while "Bah-pee" means blankie. Those are definitely two words you'll need to know if you want to build a meaningful relationship with Caleb. You also need to know that the "B-I-B" refers to the song "The B-I-B-L-E" in his hymnal, out of which he likes to sing songs daily and that "gdn-gdn" is a little board book with pictures of musical instruments. Go figure!

Although these are four of his most frequently said words during the day (other than "Mommy", "Mommy", "Mommy", "Mommy", "Mommy" ...well, you get the idea), the one that elicits the most excitement is "Gar-Be-Gar" which is, of course, Garbage Truck, and it is usually followed by "P-U"!

He used to talk about this only on Fridays when the garbage truck comes to empty the church's dumpster. Now, however, this word is spoken many times during the day...all day long...throughout the week in anticipation of the glorious day when it finally comes up our alley.

Unfortunately, we can't see the garbage truck from our back door, so when it comes, we have to actually go outside – right near the truck – so we can see and smell everything that's going on, while the sanitation engineers watch us. Am I painting you a good picture of this scene?

Anyway, Caleb has become so enamored with the "Gar-Be-Gar" that we now have to make mention of it in our prayers. You know, "Thank You, Lord for our food and our family and for the gar-be-gar." Something like that. And if we accidentally forget to mention it, he reminds us – several times – and all this with his little head bowed. How can you say "no" to that? And why should we? Right now, the "gar-be-gar" is one of Caleb's favorite things, and God wants to know the desires of our hearts. There is nothing too small or too insignificant to bring to God in prayer.

That's a good thing for us to remember. No matter how small or insignificant our prayers may be to us, they're important to God because we're important to Him. So, thank You, Father, for loving me enough to sacrifice Your Son, and thank you for my family and friends, and for sending us this special little boy to remind us of the simple things in life.

Oh, and thank You for the "gar-be-gar"!

Amusement Park Rides

Another summer has come and gone. The long days and warm nights have fled. There's a chill in the air that brings to mind sweatshirts and hot chocolate. The leaves are starting to change and Kennywood (a local amusement park) is closed for another season!

I so look forward to going to Kennywood each year. We usually go in May for the school picnic: when the weather's not too hot and there's a promise in the air of a summer that's not quite begun. And now it's all behind us. I must ask the proverbial question: Where does the time go?

I remember taking our three older children to Idlewild (another local park). Caitlin was old enough to ride the "big kid" rides, but not tall enough to do it without an adult. There's something you need to know about Chuck and me: we don't do roller coasters any more. It's not that we're afraid, it's just that we like our stomachs to stay where they belong. So, here's poor Caitlin, desperately wanting to ride the little roller coaster at Idlewild and needing an adult to go with her. I was elected! This was truly an act of love on my part. I withstood the unpredictable ups and downs for the sake of my daughter's happiness. She was thrilled to have done it and I was thrilled to be done with it! Normally, when the kids ride the roller coaster, I just wait for them at our usual meeting place: by the merry-go-round.

I like to think of myself as a merry-go-round kind of person. We always save the merry-go-round for the last ride of the night: when the lights are on. I enjoy the bright music and the gentle rhythm of the beautifully painted horses. Much more my style.

What if we compared life to an amusement park ride? If we got to choose how our life would be, I'd probably choose a merry-go-round kind of life. I'd choose a life that moves at a manageable pace. Sure, there'd be ups and downs, but they'd be expected and mild. Unfortunately, we don't always get to choose how our life will be. Sometimes we must ride the wild roller coaster of life: maybe by choice, maybe by force, maybe in support of a friend or loved one. No matter what ride we find ourselves on, we can be sure of one thing: whether it's mild or wild, someone's always in control. At Kennywood (or any amusement park), it's some kid who's working for the summer. In life, that someone is God. If we can trust some kid with our life, how much more should we be able to trust the all-knowing, all-powerful God who loves us more than we can ever imagine? When the ride seems like it's going to be too much for us, He promises that His grace is sufficient (2 Cor. 12:9) and that we can do all things by His strength (Phil. 4:13).

Even though the roller coaster is not my ride of choice, I may be called to ride it occasionally, and there may be times when I'm to simply watch others ride. If you find yourself on a wild ride, whether at an amusement park or in life, know that if I'm not on it with you, I'll be waiting for you when you get off...by the merry-go-round!

Walking Past the Bedrooms

Just a few months ago, I was able to get up on a Saturday morning before anyone else (or at least before the kids) and go downstairs passing all four bedrooms...filled with all four of my children. I remember thinking how blessed I was to have them all still at home. Charlie had graduated from college and was living at home since his dream job was only part-time. Carrie was working full time and living at home. Caitlin was just finishing up High School. And, of course, there was Caleb.

June started off with a graduation and a flight to L.A. all in the same day for Caitlin. It was a mad rush to make all of that happen. We celebrated our anniversary, Chuck went to annual conference, Caleb went to Church camp, Father's Day, Carrie's Birthday...and it was time for Caitlin to come back from her trip with the Continental Singers. A few days later, we had her graduation party, and then left for the beach. There were a few other excursions, but a lot of time went into getting Caitlin ready to go off to college. We no sooner got that over with and Charlie decided to take a new full-time job 1,000 miles away and we had two weeks to get him ready for that!

Now two of the bedrooms are empty and with Carrie working evenings, it's just the three of us for dinner...for most things. I'm comfortable with the children gone because I feel that we have given them a good foundation here at home and we talk to them on a regular basis, encouraging them in all that they do and especially in their walk with the Lord. It is my prayer that we've prepared them to be out in the world...to be in the world, but not of it.

We have a long time before all four of those bedrooms are empty and we have a life-time to continue being their parents. It doesn't matter if they're here, 1,000 miles away or somewhere in between...the relationship goes on...the love goes on.

Life goes on! I'm gearing up for my craft season and Caleb and I auditioned for and made the "Hometown Christmas" community show. I volunteered to help out in about six areas of the PTO at Caleb's school and our church is planning a huge fall activity that will occupy a good many hours in the month of October. Shopping for the holidays has already begun at our house...it just doesn't end...but that's a good thing...it's good to be busy...that way I have less time to think about how much I miss the ones who are gone...until I get up early on a Saturday morning and walk past those bedrooms, knowing two of them are empty. Yet still, I feel blessed, knowing that they are in God's hands.

Aches of a Mother

As I watch Caleb get on the school bus, I also see two of his friends...sitting with each other and leaving Caleb to sit alone. I close my eyes and I see Charlie at about the same age watching his two friends walk by our house on their way to buy more baseball cards...not stopping to see if he wants to come along. I see Carrie, kneeling by her bed at night...asking God to please give her a friend and Caitlin asking me to play yet another game because no one else wants to play with her.

Being a mother is such a blessing...but it isn't always easy. In fact, most of the time it's easily one of the hardest jobs in the world. It's easy when things are going well for your child, but when you see them being rejected or picked on...it's worse than having it happen to you. You want so much to take their hurt away...to make their lives easy...but you can't...and would you anyway if you could?

James tells us to be joyful when we face trials. In Chapter 1, he tells us that when our faith is tested, it develops perseverance which helps us to mature into the people that God wants us to be. So, even though it's unpleasant to go through trials...it's for our own good. Malachi talks about God's people going through fire...coming out shining like gold! God uses the hurts in life to make us stronger...and more like Him. When we go through difficult times, the experience gives us eyes of compassion for others who are also struggling. Another word of encouragement can be found in Romans, Chapter 8. Paul tells us that God takes all of our experiences in life...yes, even the difficult ones...and turns them into something good if we love Him and trust in Him. Also, Jesus, Himself promises to be with us...always!

So, take heart and consider it all joy when you face trials because God will be with you every step of the way and you'll come out shining like gold...my kids did!

On Being Waggled

When Carrie was a little girl, she loved to line her baby dolls up in a row and cover them with blankets...sometimes including herself! One day, she was playing in her room and I overheard her talking, rather harshly, so I took a peek and saw her scolding her row of dolls. She had one hand on her hip and the other was pointing an accusing finger (or, as a friend of mine says, "Giving the waggle"), warning her babies to stay in bed! I wondered where she learned all that...

Now, let me back up a bit. From the time Carrie became mobile, she was a climber...up the stairs, up on the furniture, out of the playpen, out of the crib. By the time she was 5, she could be seen hanging by one hand from the top of the swing set giving her best Tarzan impersonation...call and all!

Obviously during the day, I could keep an eye on her, but the nighttime scared us to death! We even thought about tying a net around the top of her crib! After several attempted escapes, I could be seen with one hand on my hip and the other with a "waggling" finger, warning her to stay in bed! I knew where she'd learned all that...from me!

Like it or not, as parents, we are the most influential people in our children's lives! Our children pick up all kinds of things from us...mannerisms, language, habits...good and bad! If our children see us reading, exercising, making healthy food choices and treating each other with love and respect, we are setting good examples for them. On the other hand, if they see us sprawled out in front of the TV all the time, a beer in one hand and a cigarette in the other, frequently getting our dinner at a drive-through and yelling at each other on a daily basis, we are also setting an example...but this time...not so good!

Now those are extreme depictions of ways that we can influence our kids, but what about the more subtle examples that we set: we regularly drive over the speed limit, we sneak candy into the movie theaters, we alter birthdates so that kids can have their own Facebook page before they're 13, we think that it's our lucky day when we get too much change back at the store...

We need to be very careful...not just as parents, but as Christians. We always need to be aware of our witness: the example that we're setting for our kids and the message that we're sending to the world around us.

In Paul's letter to Titus, he instructs Titus to set a good example in every area of his life...and that's good advice for us as well.

So, parents play with your kids and read to them. Let them see you reading your Bible and kissing in the kitchen...and praying...consider yourself "waggled"!

The Burning Bible

I was sitting in church...feeling a little under the weather, wondering what I was going to write about for this article. With my Sunday School class covered, I headed home early, anticipating a warm cup of tea on a chilly day to help me feel better. After letting myself in, I plopped down my Bible, filled the tea kettle with water, put it on the back burner and turned it on. I decided that I would tidy up the dining room while waiting for the water to boil. I was closing up the cereal box and sorting through the sections of the Sunday paper when I heard a strange noise. Thinking it was just the glass tea kettle heating up, I went about my business. As I finished my task, I looked up and saw a glow in the kitchen. I ran in to find that my Bible (which I'd plopped on the front burner) was engulfed in flames!! I realized immediately that I had mistakenly turned on the front burner instead of the back one. I quickly grabbed the Bible and threw it onto the floor. There were still 8-inch-high flames coming from the burner. I ran to the pantry, removing potatoes, flour and rice to find the fire extinguisher...only to realize that I really had no idea how to use it! I turned back toward the stove and noticed that my Bible was still burning on the floor. Thankfully, all I had to do was blow on it and it went out. Next, I said a little prayer and threw water on the burner...thus dousing the flames. What a nightmare!

Not only did I have a major mess to clean up...so much for relaxing with a cup of tea...but I had just ruined my Bible of 26 1/2 years. Now, probably only my family knows this about me, but I tend to "beat myself up" over mistakes that I make...over and over again...for years...and I had just made a "doozy"! But God knew that I was going to do this, and so He prepared me. Just that morning in my devotions, I was reading about how when we hold onto things like hatred and regret, we carry around burdens that are too heavy for us...ones that Christians have no business carrying around. Now, I don't carry around hatred and I don't hold grudges, but I have done a few things that I've regretted later on...things like giving away all the beautiful matching dresses that I made my girls and selling all of my brother's 45-rpm records in a garage sale. I bring things like that to mind on a regular basis and chastise myself for my "not-so-intelligent" decisions! (I'm trying not to use the word "stupid", but that's the kind of things I'm talking about!)

So, when I read this devotion, I prayed a prayer that God would help me not to do that anymore...and, you know, when we ask God to help us in a certain area of our lives, He often gives us tests to let us know that He's working in us...and I guess I was tested!

I have made up my mind that, with God's help, I will no longer agonize over the stupid mistakes that I've made in my life! If Moses had done that, he'd never have freed the Israelites from their bondage in Egypt, leading them to the Promised Land. If David had done that, he wouldn't have been the king whose throne will never end. If Jonah had done that, he wouldn't have turned the nation of Nineveh back to God.

God knows that we're going to make mistakes and He expects us to learn and grow from them...not wallow in them! Well, no more wallowing for me! After shedding a few tears for my Bible, I am ready (and excited) to get a new one and move on! I figure that God has some new things to teach me, some verses to show me afresh...and I'm going to need some clean, white pages so I can do some underlining and note-taking!

Just so you know, my Bible is not totally destroyed. I had a zipper cover on it, and that I'm sure, is the reason that there is still a Bible left. Both covers are gone and the top edges of the pages are singed, but as I open it up, all of my notes and thoughts are still there, waiting for me to copy them into the new Bible, if I so choose...and why should I be surprised...God makes new life out of ashes all the time!

Maps

I love going on journeys and I love using maps to make our plans! I love opening them up and finding the places where we'd like to go...tracing out the best routes with my finger. I love using the legend to see what types of roads we'll be traveling on and where various sites are, such as lighthouses and national parks, bridges and waterfalls...and even rest stops! Maps have everything you need so that you can reach your destination. Oh, I'm all in favor of using our GPS as well, especially when we're trying to get somewhere in a big city, but out on the open road...I love maps!

Maps give us instruction. They guide us along our way. They show us which road to take so that we can get to where we're going. No one forces us to follow the guidance that our maps have to offer. We have to choose to do that...or take the risk of getting lost! The only time we don't need the help of a map is when we know the way to our destination. I recently took a journey that was five hours one way and didn't use a map. I also didn't get lost...because I knew the way...I knew the way home!

We are all on a journey, whether we realize it or not. We are on the journey of life and our destination is eternity. God, who created us, has given us a map, a set of instructions to guide us along our way...to show us which road to take so that we can get to where we're going. The map that God has given us is the Bible. I love opening it up and reading the promises that God has written down for me...tracing my favorite verses with my finger. I love reading the stories of faithful men and women of God...closing my eyes and seeing the various sites, such as the Red Sea being parted and the walls of Jericho crashing to the ground, Queen Esther, who risked her life to save her people and Jesus as He preached to and fed the 5,000!

No one forces us to read the Bible...to follow the guidance that it has to offer. We have to choose to do that...or take the risk of getting lost. You see, we all have the same destination...eternity...but there are many roads and it can be very confusing. If we don't follow God's "map", we will reach our destination of eternity, but it won't be an eternity with God...we will be lost...forever! Only one way leads to an eternity with God...our faith in His saving grace provided by the death and resurrection of His Son, Jesus Christ. The Bible has everything we need so that we can reach our destination and when we read it and study it, we will know the way...we will know the way home!

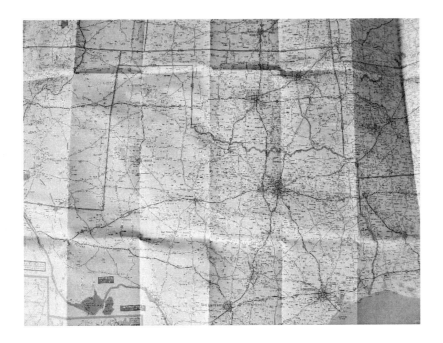

Holding Hands

One of the first things you do when you start dating is to hold hands. There's something very endearing about holding the hand of someone you care about. Chuck and I held hands a lot when we were dating. I have very fond memories of walking the campus of Grove City College, holding hands with the boy who would become the man I married. Back then, we held hands out of romantic love.

After we got married, we began to have children and with each birth, Chuck held my hand for support. As we took walks with our children, we held their hands...to keep them safe and to make sure that they stayed with us. We used our hands to tie their shoes and to wipe their tears...to hug them and to care for them. During those years, we held hands out of parental love.

Our hands are amazing! We use our hands for so many purposes. Our hands are used for healing, helping and holding. They are used for working, creating and praising God!

There are many references to hands in the Bible as well. Moses held his hands up so that Joshua could defeat the Amalekites (Exodus 17:10-13). The Israelites who lapped up water with their hands were chosen to defeat the Midianites (Judges 7:5-25). David chose to put his life in the hands of God (Psalm 31:5). Jesus' last words from the cross were committing His spirit into His Father's hands (Luke 23:46). Now, Jesus sits at the right hand of His Father in Heaven...promising to be with us always...holding us in the palm of His hand with godly love.

We are now empty-nesters and when we take walks, we hold hands out of romantic love, but also to steady each other...especially when hiking on uneven ground. Last Sunday afternoon, Chuck and I spent a couple of hours at Idlewild Park...one last time before they close for the season. I enjoyed walking through the fallen leaves with the autumn sunshine on our faces...holding hands with that boy once again out of a lifetime of love!

One Beautiful Love Story

All Scripture is God-breathed and is useful for teaching, rebuking, correcting and training in righteousness, so that the man of God may be thoroughly equipped for every good work." ~2 Timothy 3:16

There are some heavy-duty Christian thinkers who have suggested that, as Christians, we no longer have need of the Old Testament. They argue that Jesus came to fulfill the Old Testament prophecies and with Him began the age of a new covenant between man and God – all of which is true, but it doesn't mean that we don't need the Old Testament. My wise husband put it this way: "We learn from the Old Testament and we live by the New."

God's Word is all one beautiful love story between a Creator-God and His people. From the very beginning He created us to be in relationship with Him and gave us a free will to choose to have a perfect relationship with Him or not. Adam and Eve chose the latter and ever since that time, God has been orchestrating a plan to restore that broken relationship to its original perfection.

God promised in Genesis 3:15 that one day, Eve's child would crush the serpent's head by defeating death. Throughout the Old Testament, God reminds us of His promised Messiah. 4,000 years after that promise, Jesus enters our world, eventually defeating death and fulfilling God's plan to restore our relationship with Him.

Today, we all have that same free will: to choose to have an eventually perfect relationship with Him or not. So, "Choose for yourselves this day whom you will serve. As for me and my household, we will serve the Lord." ~Joshua 24:15

I've spent my entire adult life teaching children, my own and those in Sunday school, about Jesus and His love for them. God made His good news (the Gospel) easy enough for a child to understand. In fact, Jesus said in Matthew 18:3, "I tell you the truth, unless you change and become like little children, you will never enter the Kingdom of Heaven."

Let's not over-think the Gospel. Realize that all Scripture is a gift from God and use it to make the right choice – choose to be in a right relationship with God and one day, when you get to Heaven, it will be perfect!

Don't Forget to Water

Upon returning back home from one of our trips this summer, I found that some of our potted flowers out back had not received any water while we were gone. They were parched and withered and I could have easily given up on them, but I didn't. I watered them and didn't notice any immediate change; however, after a few days of watering and pruning, they seemed to be coming back. Now, they're back to the way they were before we left.

We, too, need water to live but as Christians, we also need Living Water. Jesus refers to Living Water in John's Gospel as the Holy Spirit and says that He will give to those who ask. In other words, unlike my plants, which are at my mercy, we can, and must, initiate the spiritual "watering" process. We can either choose to be "watered" or choose not to be. When we deprive ourselves of the Living Water, we begin to wither and become parched and eventually die. Just as those flowers desperately needed the water I gave them, we, as Christians, desperately need the Living Water that only Jesus can give.

The good news is that, just as I didn't give up on those flowers, Jesus never gives up on us! One word of caution: although the flowers are doing well now, had they received the proper care the entire summer, they would be doing much better at this point in time. Likewise, if we allow ourselves to go through the process of being deprived and revived, we'll pay a price. Avoid such a setback! Choose to receive your daily dose of Living Water and flourish under the care of your Savior!

"Ode To a Friend"

Our family recently lost a good friend. She was the perfect definition of a friend: Loyal, faithful and true. Proverbs 17:17 says that, "A friend loves at all times." And her love was all that and more. Her love for us was unconditional. Our lives are busy and whether we had a lot of time to give or a little, she gladly accepted what we had to offer. Her entire existence was defined by the time she was able to spend with us. Our family was the apple of her eye. This love, however, was not reserved for only our family. She extended her love to everyone she met. Anyone we welcomed into our home, was equally welcomed by our friend. You see, our friend was also a member of the family. She was our dog, Lou.

Lou was not perfect by any means. There was the time she ate a whole pound of chocolate discs that had been purchased for Christmas baking. They didn't agree with her…well, we won't get into that. We also have lovely blue furniture in our living room because the beige chair had a huge hole chewed in it when we went away for Thanksgiving. She also had a habit of greeting all of our guests with her own special blessing. (Those of you who knew Lou know exactly what I'm referring to!) No, she wasn't perfect, but she was ours and we loved her even with her faults…as she did us.

Friends and family members come and go on this earth and that is so hard to deal with. To me, it would be impossible to deal with if we didn't have the One True Friend who is always with us: Jesus. He, too, loves us unconditionally and desires nothing more than to spend time with us. He, however, is perfect: eternal…everlasting. His love is not reserved for a few, but is extended to everyone. Earthly friends (be they people or pets) are a blessing from God and bring us happiness in life. Friendship with God brings us life itself. May your life be blessed with many friends, but especially with the One True Friend…Jesus.   P.S. Lou – we love you and miss you.

Scrapbooks & Remembering

Well, I'm finally making a scrapbook for our trip out west. I've never made this kind of scrapbook before...you know, the ones that are all the rage? I've thought about making one for a long time, but just wasn't interested until now. I remember the different papers and special scissors that were available when I used to work at JoAnn Fabrics (7 years ago)! I don't know if you've been in a craft store lately...they have aisles (plural) for this stuff! It's overwhelming!

I had an idea of what to get...a book with page protectors, an assortment of stylish papers (12x12 size), stickers and some of those special scissors. I also happened to pick up a book, "Scrapbooking for Dummies", that I figured might come in handy.

As I began to read the book, I found out that I also needed a glue dispenser (that takes refills) and some special journaling pens, "pigment ink, acid free, archival quality, waterproof, fadeproof, non-bleeding"! That's quite a mouthful for a fine point magic marker!

So, here I am...building this book page by page (each page has to tell its own story) and although it's a lot of fun using all the neat materials, the most fun is the remembering. Remembering the sight and the emotions that went along with seeing such amazing things for the first time. Thank goodness I kept a journal! As I read back through my notes, I'm reminded of things that after only two months, I'd forgotten. How quickly we forget...even when it's something important...something we should remember or want to remember. Remembering things from our past shapes our lives in the present and future.

God is "big" on remembering. He says in Exodus 20:8, "Remember the Sabbath day." Deuteronomy 5:15, "Remember that you were slaves in Egypt." 1 Chronicles 16:12, "Remember the wonders He has done."

He also knows that it is difficult for us to remember all the things we should. In Deuteronomy 6:4-9, He gives us some commandments and tells us that they are to be on our hearts. "Impress them on your children. Talk about them when you sit at home and when you walk along the road, when you lie down and when you get up. Tie them as symbols on your hands and bind them on your foreheads. Write them on the doorframes of your houses and on your gates."

I like to imagine that if God were giving these instructions today, He'd tell the people to make a scrap or *memory* book out of their past. Something that they would enjoy looking at for years to come!

P.S. Dear Moses, when you're making that book, don't forget to put in a picture of the parting of the Red Sea as well as the water coming out of a rock and remember...every page has to tell a story!

Books, Books, Books

All we wanted to do was tidy up a bit...find a place to put a few things...when one thing led to another...like a domino effect...an uncontrollable chain of events!

Caleb likes to draw and he had quite a few pages of drawings that he wanted to save...where to save them was the problem. In his room, he has 3 stackable toy bins with 3 drawers each...all full! He has shelves and a toy box in his closet...all full! He has six furniture drawers and three bookshelves...you guessed it...all full!

We found some books in one of the desk drawers and reasoned that if they could be put on a shelf in the bookcase, there would be room in that drawer for some of his drawing materials, which would empty out another drawer that could be used for the drawings that he wanted to save...phew! Please tell me that you've been here before and that I'm not alone in this madness!

Anyway, in order to begin this process, we needed to remove some of the books from his already-full bookcase...but which ones? Since he's entering the 4th grade and now reads mostly chapter books, we decided to move the row of story books that he'd been hanging on to. Most of the younger books had already found other homes...keepsake books are in a bin in the attic and some favorites like, "Are You My Mother", "Horton Hears a Who" and "The Velveteen Rabbit" are in the living room. There's also a whole shelf in the guest room devoted to stories about Babar, the Cat in the Hat and Winnie the Pooh.

I found myself making room on one of the already-full shelves in the guest room for these books that he finally decided to relinquish. The only place I could find was on the very top shelf...definitely out of Caleb's reach. As I began to place them up on the shelf, I felt as if I was saying goodbye to some old friends! I could see us cuddled up under a blanket as we read about the antics of the "Berenstain Bears who lived in the big tree house down a sunny dirt road deep in Bear

Country". I could hear Chuck reading yet another "Little Critter" book following the nightly wrestling match that had just taken place on Caleb's bed. I could see Caleb's eyes light up as we read about Buzz Lightyear taking flight and hear his little laugh when we found Curious George getting into trouble again!

When I mentioned earlier that we were caught in an uncontrollable chain of events, I wasn't just referring to the process of transferring "stuff" from one place to another...I was also thinking about the unstoppable, inevitable growing up of a child. Being a Mom is a very complicated thing...I can have tears in my eyes as I cherish the memories of when my children were young while being filled with exceeding joy as I watch them grow into the men and women that God intends for them to be. 1 Corinthians 13:11 says, "When I was a child, I talked like a child, I thought like a child, I reasoned like a child. When I became a man, I put childish ways behind me."

Such is the way of life...ever-changing...one thing leading to another...I wouldn't have it any other way...would you?

P.S. If you ever want to borrow any books...

The Potato Incident

I t's true what they say: "No matter how old your kids get, they're still your kids." Three out of four of our children are out on their own, but whenever we see them, we like to buy them groceries and other small items that they need...we can't help it...they're still our kids!

This past March, we headed down to Richmond to see Charlie and we did just that. We brought things for the fridge like milk, eggs and butter. We brought things for the cupboard like canned goods, cereal and pasta. We brought frozen items, produce and, of course, freshly baked cookies! One of the produce items was a 5# bag of potatoes. Charlie found a place for everything...putting the potatoes in one of those cupboards that you seldom use because they're too hard to reach...

Earlier in the summer, as the temperature started to rise, Charlie noticed an odor in his kitchen that went from odd to disturbing to unbearable! He took out the trash and cleaned everything in sight to no avail. Finally, he began looking in cupboards and, lo and behold, found what USED to be a 5# bag of potatoes! (Which I'm sure you'd already guessed!) He got them out of the house and scrubbed the cupboard and things were back to normal!

We've had some laughs over the "Potato Incident" and I've recalled it several times over the summer. I've thought how if Charlie had been able to locate the source of the odor when he first noticed it, he would've been spared a lot of unnecessary work and aggravation! Or, if he'd paid attention to the potatoes sooner, he could've gotten rid of the rotten one that started the whole thing (because that's usually how it happens) and been able to put the rest of the potatoes to good use.

I've also thought about how that "Potato Incident" mirrors our lives. If we keep our lives in check, we will be aware when something rotten is present...when some sin is crouching at the door (see Genesis 4:7). We will then be able to remove the sin...the bad attitude, the disobedience, the unfaithfulness...whatever it is that is rotten within us and get our lives back in order so that we can be of good use to God!

Let's make sure that our lives aren't in some "seldom-used cupboard". We need to be reading God's Word daily and taking every opportunity to be in His house...worshipping Him and growing in our faith...keeping ourselves accountable to other believers so that no sin can take root in our lives...spoiling us for any good use!

Preparing for School

A new pair of shoes. Check. A new backpack (well, it's actually a messenger bag). Check. A new binder, some folders, a jump drive for computer class and some graphite for his mechanical pencils. Check. An assortment of new jeans, shorts and shirts. Check. A variety of foods to put in a sack lunch on the days that he packs. Check. It takes a lot to prepare Caleb (and any student, for that matter) to head back to school...although, not as much as it did when I was sending all four of the kids!

The list appears to be complete. It doesn't seem that we've left anything out...at least not at first glance. Preparing your child for school includes more than some new clothes and school supplies. It also includes things like prayer, Bible reading, encouragement and support. As adults, we know how hard life can be at times and that's true for our children too. We need to be more than physically and intellectually ready to face the day. We need to be spiritually ready as well!

So, let me share a bit of our school-morning routine:

- Before the morning, we make sure that there is an appropriate bed-time.
- We get up a little over an hour before bus time so that we're not rushed.
- Caleb gets dressed & makes his bed before coming downstairs...at a set time.
- His breakfast is waiting for him when he gets downstairs. We have a prayer, devotions and then enjoy part of a book that we're reading together.
- With 20 minutes left, he takes his dishes to the sink and heads to the bathroom for his grooming...etc. while I pack his lunch.
- As he leaves, we encourage him to do his best and to remember who he is...that is, a Christian!

Throughout the day, he comes to mind...as do all of our kids...and we offer up prayers for protection and that they will be ever-growing closer to Him...lights shining in a dark world!

I hope that this will be an encouragement to you and a source of help for those "sometimes hectic" mornings.

Love Notes

September is back to school time. The end of summer vacation, almost as much shopping as Christmas! Well, it isn't so bad now with just Caleb living at home and going to school, but not too many years ago we were getting sometimes three, sometimes four kids ready to go back to school...needing shoes, clothes, backpacks, school supplies and a variety of lunch containers over the years...not to mention all the food to go in them! I've packed a lot of lunches in everything from lunch boxes sporting Mickey Mouse or the Ghostbusters to mini coolers to brown bags. These lunches have contained sandwiches ranging from turkey and cheese to bologna to egg salad to the ever-popular PB & J! They always had some sort of fruit, a snack and dessert...usually a homemade cookie. For drinks, we started with thermoses and then went to juice boxes and eventually ended up with them purchasing milk at school...chocolate, which was a rare treat! Yes, the "sack" lunch has had many variations over the years, but there's one thing they all had in common...they all had a paper napkin...with a note!

Kids spend a lot of hours away from home at school and it isn't always a pleasant experience. The bus can be rough and classes can be difficult. The cafeteria can be a lonely place...which is why I many times included a note with that sack lunch. I would say things like, "Have a nice day!" or "I love you!" Sometimes, when I knew they had a tough test coming up that afternoon, I would remind them that I was praying for them. Sometimes I would just draw a smiley face or a heart...just so they would remember that someone loves them! One of the best things about being a parent is to be able to let your children know that you love them unconditionally...just the way they are!

I have to confess...the idea of leaving a "love" note is not my idea...God did it first. You see, He realizes that living here on earth isn't always a pleasant experience. Life can be rough and difficult and lonely...and so He gave us a note...the Bible...His

Word...just so we would remember that Someone loves us!
And one of the best things about our Heavenly Father is that
He loves us unconditionally...just the way we are!

35th Anniversary

We had an amazing trip to California to celebrate our 35th Anniversary! We saw everything from the tall, majestic redwoods to the gigantic sequoias. We were lulled to sleep at night by the crashing waves of the Pacific and awakened in the morning by the sound of the gulls greeting the new day. We climbed a mountain and walked across the Golden Gate Bridge. We hopped on and off of the cable cars, meeting people from Germany, France, England, Scotland, Australia and China...and from right here in Pennsylvania! We re-kindled our love as it was when we first met...holding hands and listening to some of our old songs. Our energy was high and our spirits were soaring!

One morning, as we were sharing our plans for the day with a hotel employee behind the desk, she said how much she loved our excitement about the things that we were going to do and her colleague confessed that he hadn't gone into San Francisco for over three years and hadn't even bothered to visit some of the places that we were planning to see.

I thought about their comments throughout the day and I realized that, as Christians, we can become like that where our faith is concerned. We allow the busyness of our daily routine to distract us from noticing the beauty of God's creation that is all around us. We should be so excited to share God's plan for salvation with those we meet...so excited about God's love for us that others take notice of our excitement and want to know more!

Our vacation was like a breath of fresh air with all the excitement of a first love...our love! May we all breathe the fresh air of the Holy Spirit and may our faith be strengthened and renewed. May our love for the Lord be re-kindled and may our excitement be contagious!

I Love Fall

I love fall! Fall is comfort food and pumpkin patches. Fall is kids playing in the colorful leaves that have covered the ground. Fall is taking a hike in your most comfortable sweatshirt and enjoying hot chocolate from a thermos. Fall is also my favorite season to decorate the house.

Decorating for fall is a big project. First, I have to gather up and put away all of the summer decorations and then I enlist my big, strong husband to bring up everything for fall (4 bins and 3 big bags). The first thing I do is open the bin containing all of my fall candles. I lift the lid and my senses explode with the scents of cinnamon, pumpkin and spice...making sure that I am definitely ready to decorate for fall!

Another thing I love about fall is how so many of my decorations remind me to be thankful. I don't decorate for Halloween, so my fall decorations are more about the harvest and colorful leaves and Thanksgiving. As I place each treasured item around the house, I find myself giving thanks for all the blessings in my life!

It's good to surround ourselves with things that make us think about God...things that remind us of His beautiful creation...things that inspire us to praise and thank Him...even things with Scripture on them to help us learn His Word.

Whether you decorate for fall or just enjoy getting outside to enjoy God's decorations, remember to be thankful and to praise Him for all that He does and all that He is...One who loves you!

Communion Prayer

I look forward to taking communion each month. It's such a powerful reminder of what Jesus did for us: how He loved us enough to offer Himself up as a payment for our sins; how He loved us enough to go through so much pain and shame so that we could have the opportunity to regain a right relationship with God...if we choose to follow Him.

For the longest time, I would take communion and then I would spend the rest of that time with head bowed and eyes closed, thanking God for His amazing provision, but a few years ago, I realized that there was something else I could be doing during that time. I realized that I could be praying for the other people around me who were also taking communion.

I sit up front and am usually one of the first to take communion, and then I hurriedly return to my seat and lift folks up in prayer as they file past my pew. I only have a few seconds for each person, so I just lift them up by mentioning their names and trust that God knows their needs. Occasionally, someone comes forward whose name I don't know, which prompts me to find out who they are. I consider this to be a sort of ministry to the people in our congregation and I encourage you to join me in this venture. James tells us to "pray for each other" in chapter 5, verse 16 and he also says that "The prayer of a righteous [man] is powerful and effective."

In two weeks, we will celebrate communion again on World Communion Sunday. It's important to get to know the people who are part of our church family and one of the best ways to begin that relationship is to pray for them!

Groceries and Grace

Shopping for groceries is a complicated business for the conscientious consumer. It involves coupon clipping, scanning several weekly sale fliers, making lists for each store and strategically combining shopping trips with other errands in order to save on gas. I do all of this in order to be a good steward of our finances and because we need to have sufficient funds left over to meet our other needs.

Reckless spending in one area of the budget can seriously affect other areas in an unfortunate way. That's why I'm *usually* very careful to stick to my lists and to think through thoroughly before making any purchases. Impulsive buying can be very dangerous. Did you notice that I said, "usually?"

Let me tell you about a time recently when an impulsive purchase got me into trouble.

Carrie and I were picking up a few things at Giant Eagle. Giant Eagle is one of those big grocery stores that has a little café right in the store where you can eat your breakfast or lunch. It's always crowded, but I've never indulged. Remember, when I'm grocery shopping, I'm on a mission!

It was after school, and I'd had a busy day and hadn't yet decided what to make for dinner. I was out of ideas and rapidly running out of time when we happened upon the café where they had a Chinese food bar. I'd noticed it before, briefly taking in the nice variety, but really hadn't paid a whole lot of attention to it.

That afternoon as I gazed at the fried rice and the sweet and sour chicken, I decided, impulsively, that this would make an excellent dinner. I took note of the price ($4.99) and asked the lady selling chicken how to go about getting some Chinese food to take home. She pointed to the plastic containers and told me to fill one of those and pay for it in the café. Sounded simple enough and for $4.99, I decided that we'd get two containers.

So, Carrie and I each took one and I told her to fill it as full as she could with as many different kinds of food as she could so that we could get our money's worth. Remember, I am the conscientious consumer!

We heaped our containers, barely able to fasten the lids. We'd done ourselves proud. We took it over to the register and I took out a $10 bill and told her that we had two containers. She smiled at me and told me to put them on the scale. (Now, just as it is polite to let someone finish telling you a joke you've already heard, if you've figured out where this story is headed, it would be polite to quit laughing and let me finish!) I gently placed our two bulging containers on the scale and she politely smiled again and said, "That will be $27.88."

I tried to maintain a calm and collected façade as I emptied out my wallet, and then I steered Carrie back over to the Chinese food bar to share with her the very important lesson I had just learned. I pointed to the sign which read (you guessed it) $4.99 A POUND and told her that I had failed to notice the pound (#) sign.

As I wandered in a daze through the rest of the store attempting to pick up the things that were actually on my list, I kept saying over and over, "I can't believe I did that and your father is not going to believe it either." I wasn't afraid that he'd be angry, but I was embarrassed to have to admit that I'd made such a stupid mistake and that I'd wasted so much money! I'm the one who always gets the good bargains!

Needless to say, when we got home, I relayed the whole sordid tale (Carrie was only too happy to chime in) and instead of being reprimanded or laughed at, I was hugged and told that it was okay, and that the food would be delicious!

You see, Chuck knew that I was well aware of my mistake and that he didn't need to point it out. He also knew that he needed to be careful not to make me feel any worse than I already did.

Webster defines grace as unmerited favor. That is what Chuck gave me and that is what God gives to us. When we are truly sorry for what we've done, God greets us with a hug and tells us that everything will be okay. That is also how we should treat one another. Matthew 6:14-15 says, "For if you forgive men when they sin against you, your Heavenly Father will also forgive you. But, if you do not forgive men their sins, your Father will not forgive your sins."

We all make mistakes. Let us follow Christ's example and be forgiving and full of grace. Anyone for Chinese? I'M NOT BUYING!

Micah James

Micah James was born on Monday, June 1, 2015...blessing us with grandchild #4 and giving us two of each!

He and Carrie came home from the hospital on Wednesday and he had a lot to get used to...his big sister, Emily and his big brother, Daniel. He also met his first dog and cats...all in his brand new surroundings...home!

During one of his diaper changes, he began to cry...and I mean cry...he was seriously stressed! We tried giving him a pacifier and talking to him...everyone took their turn trying to console him to no avail...everyone except Carrie. Finally, she walked over to him and put her hand by his face and he calmed down immediately! We were all amazed! He smelled her scent and felt her touch...and an instant peace washed over him.

That's how our relationship with God should be. Lots of things in life can cause us to be stressed...our job, the housework, the kids, our finances...the list is endless. And we usually try to find comfort and peace in anyone or anything except God.

Jesus is the Prince of Peace and throughout the Gospels, He promises to give us peace. When we spend time reading His Word and in His presence in prayer, He promises to give us peace...a peace that surpasses all understanding.

As Carrie's presence was the solution to Micah's stress, being in God's presence is the solution to ours. Spend quality time with God this summer and be at peace!

Surprise at the Theater

A few days ago, Chuck, Caleb and I went to see the new Captain America movie. We picked Caleb up at the end of school in order to catch the matinee. Our theater of choice was just a little too far away and we were afraid that we were going to miss the beginning of the movie, so we went to a smaller venue because it was closer...figuring that it was better to sacrifice the quality of the larger theater than to walk in when the movie had already started. We were met with a couple of surprises: first of all, the screen wasn't any smaller than the other theater's and they played the movie just for the three of us...no one else showed up for that particular matinee!

I'll have to admit that it felt a little weird being the only ones in the theater. I half expected them to come in and tell us that the movie wouldn't be shown as advertised due to a lack of interest! But, when the time came around for the show to begin, they kept their word and the movie began, as promised!

After a while I was used to fact that we were alone in the theater...and I found myself actually liking the idea. You see, when I watch a movie, I really get involved in the plot and with the characters. I jump right on the emotional roller coaster that the director builds when they are filming the movie...laughing, crying, oohing and aahing in all the right places...and that can be embarrassing in front of other people. But yesterday, I didn't have to worry about that!

After we left the theater, I started thinking about how our experience was a little like our relationship with God. Just as we were surprised by how big the screen was, we are often surprised by how big our God is. We tend to think of Him in human terms, but when we get a glimpse of who He really is and how He really is...we're surprisingly amazed! And, just as we weren't sure if they were going to show the movie for a measly three people, it's hard to believe that Jesus would've died just for me. It's easier to believe that He left Heaven and the company of the Father in order to save the whole world...but just for me? That's hard to imagine! But the Bible tells us that He loves each and every one of us individually...so much so that He knew us before we were formed (See Psalm 139:13-16). We just forget that sometimes!

We need to remember how precious we are in His sight and that we can be completely comfortable around Him...laughing, crying, oohing and aahing as we ride the roller coaster of this life that He built for us...knowing that at the end of the ride, we'll be welcomed with open arms to our heavenly home by our Heavenly Father...just as He promised!

Cherish Every Moment

So, I decided to make scrapbooks for Charlie, Carrie & Caitlin for Christmas. Their pictures had fallen out of their "sticky page" albums which had obviously lost their "stickiness". I knew it was going to be a big job, so I started at the end of August when Caleb went back to school. I went shopping for books, themed 12 x 12 paper, card stock, cutting implements & countless related stickers & glue sticks. I sorted through hundreds of pictures...making copies when necessary... creating baby, childhood & family pages as well as pages for holidays, vacations and school days. I ended each book with a personal letter and, long story short...260 pages & 4 months later (I finished on Christmas morning!), I had completed the project and had, what I felt to be, a meaningful gift to give!

It was very nostalgic looking back through all of that "growing up"...wondering how time went so fast! To say that it was an emotional time for me would be an extreme understatement! All of the pictures I used were great...fancy dresses, special occasions, new bicycles...but some of the best were every-day shots...Charlie getting ready to push baby sister,

All are special in their own way

Carrie, in the stroller...Carrie in her playhouse with her dolls...~2-year-old Caitlin all dressed up in big brother's jacket, hat & shoes...so pleased that she had accomplished it all by herself! Some of the pages were very fancy and some were plainer...kind of like life...but all are special in their own way. I've never been more relieved to have a project finished...but I've also never been gladder to have done it.

As I look back on the past, I know that there were many days that I took for granted...days when I went through the motions...not appreciating each moment that I had to spend with loved ones. We can never get those moments back...and some of our loved ones are gone, but we do have wonderful memories & we do have the future. If I learned anything from making these books, I learned that we need to cherish the time that we can spend with people we love...being thankful for each & every moment that God had given us.

While this is the end of this book, it is not the end of the story. If you enjoyed this collection of Ponderings, please consider donating to help us publish a sequel or two of Cheryl's writings.

More information is available at:

www.PonderingsFromThePastorsPartner.com

Thank you and God Bless!